COPING
WITH YOUR
ANGER

Published by The Westminster Press

By Andrew D. Lester
   Pastoral Care with Children in Crisis
   Coping with Your Anger: A Christian Guide

By Andrew D. and Judith L. Lester
   Understanding Aging Parents (Christian Care Books)

Edited by Gerald L. Borchert and Andrew D. Lester
   Spiritual Dimensions of Pastoral Care:
   Witness to the Ministry of Wayne E. Oates

COPING

WITH YOUR

ANGER

A Christian Guide

by

Andrew D. Lester

THE WESTMINSTER PRESS
Philadelphia

Scripture quotations from the Revised Standard Version of the Bible are copyrighted 1946, 1952, © 1971, 1973 by the Division of Christian Education of the National Council of the Churches of Christ in the U.S.A., and are used by permission.

BOOK DESIGN BY ALICE DERR

Published by The Westminster Press ®
Philadelphia, Pennsylvania

PRINTED IN THE UNITED STATES OF AMERICA
9 8 7 6

Library of Congress Cataloging in Publication Data

Lester, Andrew D.
  Coping with your anger.

  Bibliography: p.
  1. Anger—Religious aspects—Christianity.
2. Christian life—1960–   . I. Title.
BV4627.A5L47 1983   241'.3   82-24730
ISBN 0–664–24471–8 (pbk.)

To Wayne E. Oates
who first taught me how
to deal creatively with anger

Contents

Preface

My work in ministry, particularly when I am functioning as a pastoral counselor, puts me in touch with many people who are unable to push further toward "abundant life" because they are so anxious about anger. As a result of this anxiety, they ignore anger, or pretend they really don't get angry (or frustrated, or hurt, or disappointed). Then this unrecognized anger is expressed in a destructive manner, causing much harm to friendships, groups, and marriage and family relationships.

This anxiety about anger is often based on the idea that "Christians shouldn't get angry." This belief has a long history among Christians, but is basically *not true*. One purpose of this book is to reexamine what the Christian faith has to say on the subject of anger. Another purpose is to present a method by which Christians can cope more creatively and lovingly with anger.

I am grateful to those persons who have invited me to share their struggles with anger. Some of them have graciously permitted me to include part of their experience in these pages. Although names are changed, everything else in the illustration uses their actual story.

A number of friends and colleagues have generously read different pieces and phases of this manuscript and have provided valuable feedback. Furthermore, I am indebted to those seminary students, pastors, and lay people who have joined me in the study of anger through classes, seminars, and workshops. Their responses, insights, and personal experiences have helped me develop and "fine tune" the ideas in this book.

Judy, my wife, and Scott and Denise, my children, have been understanding of my use of family time to complete this project. When the final manuscript went to the post office they treated me to a special celebration dinner. They have joined me in working to experience and express anger in ways that contribute to, rather than destroy, the intimacy of our family.

A.D.L.

Chapter 1
Anger Reconsidered

Anger is not a nice word. It has a poor reputation in our society, particularly in the church. Many Christians put anger in the same category as lying, stealing, cheating, and using profanity. Although anger is related to positive values, such as justice, self-defense, and independence, it seems to travel more often in the wrong company—violence, fighting, yelling, and punishment, for example. Therefore society holds anger guilty by association.

It is no wonder that you and I feel uncomfortable when we are around anger. Last night in a restaurant where I was eating, a loud argument began in another room. I noticed that my stomach tightened and it was hard to concentrate on the conversation at my table. What about you? When you hear anger expressed do you feel ill at ease?

A friend recently explained his absence at a church business meeting with the comment, "I knew there would be conflict over the personnel committee recommendations and I just didn't have the heart for it." What about you? When you sense conflict do you get anxious and try to avoid it? If you do get caught in a situation where anger is expressed, do you try to smooth things over with something like, "Now, now, we shouldn't argue"?

Discomfort may become embarrassment if the anger is yours. If you think good people don't get angry, then your own anger will make you really feel uptight. You will feel terrible after getting angry, because you will believe that you did something wrong and are a bad person. In short, you will feel guilty!

WHY DO WE FEEL GUILTY?

Why do you and I feel so uncomfortable around anger? Why do we feel guilty when we feel angry? Three reasons are obvious: (1) social expectations to be "nice," (2) bad experiences with anger, and (3) Christianity's idea that anger is bad.

BEING "NICE"

Our society worships "being nice." To be thought of as a nice person is important. It has become a desirable personality trait. "Isn't she the nicest person!" and "He's really a nice guy!" are accepted as statements of high praise.

What does "being nice" mean? At best, it means being friendly, polite, and thoughtful. But the most important ingredient is to *never be angry!* To qualify, you must never appear upset, irritated, or angry. Furthermore, it is necessary to smile constantly, even when you are mad, because nice people do not confront, enter into conflict, or "make waves."

When niceness became a valued characteristic, parents became more concerned to raise their children accordingly. Therefore, any words or actions judged "not nice" are frowned upon by parents. A common parental response, one you and I heard often as children, is "That's not nice!" You heard this comment if your parents caught you sticking out your tongue, letting your underwear show, spitting, wiping your nose on your sleeve, giggling at the fat lady, making fun of the kid next door, or using "bathroom language." But you really heard it if you acted or spoke angrily! You couldn't push your sister down, hit your brother, fight, get mad, raise your voice, pout, slam the door, or use curse words. (Have you ever stopped to consider the relationship of cursing to anger? One reason the church doesn't like curse words is that they express anger.)

If a child in most families dares to get angry with a brother or a sister, what does the child hear? "Shame on you!" or, "You shouldn't feel that way about your sister." Even stronger is the response to the child who dares to get angry with a parent, "Don't talk that way to me!" The child learns several lessons in a hurry: (1) It is not "nice" to get angry. (2) Only bad kids get angry. (3) I won't be loved, or even liked, if I get angry. So what does the child conclude? "I won't be loved by my family and friends if I get angry!"

"Being nice" wasn't just necessary at home when you and I grew up. Schoolteachers thought you should be nice, too, and any angry behavior brought about a warning and then punishment (often done in anger, of course!). We also had to be nice boys and girls in Sunday school, where we learned about that sweet man, Jesus. (They forgot to tell us that Jesus got angry!) So we learned that being angry was not right. We came to believe that "good" people from "good" families do not speak or act in angry ways. Now, as adults, we try not to let ourselves show any anger.

Please understand that I am not against honest friendliness, thoughtfulness, politeness, understanding, caring, and so forth. However, being nice too often means hiding angry feelings behind plastic smiles in order to deceive others. It leads to dishonest communication about emotions. At worst, it leads people to suppress their angry feelings until all their emotions are frozen. They lose the ability to express any feelings, including joy, grief, and passion, as well as anger.

BAD EXPERIENCES WITH ANGER

To be exposed to someone's anger can be a scary, disturbing experience. You may have had some bad experiences with anger in the past which contribute to the fear you feel about anger now.

Pam Johnson, twenty-eight, and Robert Caldwell, thirty-four, were in the same small counseling group. They shared a similar struggle because Pam's father had been an alcoholic and Robert's mother had been a problem drinker. Both Pam and Robert had experienced destructive outbursts of anger from a drunken parent. Pam's father had been very happy when sober, but when drunk he had often abused her with his belt or with the long chain of keys he carried to work. Robert had dreaded coming home from school, never knowing when his mother would have had too much to drink. "When she had," Robert said, "the whole house would shake with her yelling and screaming." Both had been frightened by their experience and had sworn they would not be angry as adults. Pam had vowed never to lay a hand on a child, and Robert had vowed never to raise his voice.

Pam and Robert were in this group because their unwillingness to feel any emotion, particularly anger, was interfering with their function as spouses and parents. The early experiences taught them to fear anger. To succeed in squelching their anger, however, they had to cut off all emotion. They had lost the ability to express feelings, which made it difficult for their spouses and children to relate to them. A person who can't feel is not completely human. Emotions (joy, grief, passion, as well as anger) are necessary to living an abundant life.

We can also have negative experiences with our own anger. This happened to me in the seventh grade.

When Ira moved into our school, he was the only boy in my class smaller than I was. I was glad to see him, but he picked on me constantly. His favorite trick was to jump on my back when I wasn't looking. I tried to ignore him, be nice to him, and avoid fighting. But one day when Ira jumped on my back, my stored-up anger exploded into action quicker than I could control it. I threw him over my head onto the basketball court and began to beat his head on the asphalt. When the coach finally pulled me off, I was shaking with rage and fear.

You can imagine how ashamed I, with my upbringing, felt for "losing my temper." I don't think I ever told my parents about it. I was truly sorry for causing the cuts and bruises. Most significantly for my future, however, I promised myself never to get that angry again! I became afraid of my anger. No one helped me understand that my anger was appropriate and justified, even if my actions were questionable.

Your discomfort with being angry may be rooted in some event which left you afraid of your own anger. In any case, your past experiences with anger affect how you think and feel about anger as an adult. It would be helpful if you paused for a moment and remembered these events. What happened? How did you feel about yourself afterward? What did you decide about anger?

CHRISTIANITY SAYS ANGER IS BAD

Many Christians have been taught that anger in any shape or form is sinful. This is perhaps the most significant reason you and I feel guilty about anger. Underneath our society's suspicion of anger lie centuries of Christian teaching that anger is evil. Anger has been discounted as part of our "carnal nature" and representative of human depravity. In the Middle Ages anger became identified as one of the seven deadly sins. Fervent sermons have traced anger back to the Fall and suggested that if it were not for original sin, human beings would not be plagued by anger at all. We shall discover in Chapter 3 that *anger originates in creation,* not in the Fall. We will see that its roots are in our basic humanness rather than our sinfulness.

Furthermore, Scripture has been read with the above prejudice, so that only those biblical passages which describe destructive anger are quoted. From preachers and devotional books you have learned that anger separates one from God ("the dividing wall of hostility"—Eph. 2:14), does not contribute to the Kingdom of God ("the anger of man does not work the righteousness of God"—James 1:20), and is equal to murder ("But I say to you that every one who is angry with his brother shall be liable to judgment"—Matt. 5:22). These passages, and others, are presented as unquestionable proof that Christians should not feel angry. When we reexamine what the Bible says about anger in Chapter 3, we will find quite a different perspective.

CHALLENGING THE MISUNDERSTANDING ABOUT ANGER

The idea that anger is a bad, sinful emotion has developed over many centuries. During this time many misunderstandings have developed. In this book I will challenge these misunderstandings and provide some needed correctives.

One misunderstanding of the nature of anger is represented by the person who says, "I never get angry." Some Christians believe that if you work at it (by counting to ten, praying without ceasing, or thinking positive thoughts), you can keep yourself from feeling angry. Some Christian traditions teach that reaching "sanctification" or "perfection" in the spiritual life means eliminating all "negative" emotion, such as anger.

The truth is that *every human being experiences anger!* Yes, even Christians. No one can live throughout life without frequently experiencing this emotion. Why? Because anger is a part of our human nature. God has created us this way! We will discuss where anger comes from in the next chapter and explain why all humans feel angry.

It is possible to work so hard at not having any anger that you can block out the *feeling* of anger. Some of you may truthfully say, "I don't get angry." This means that you have used mental tricks to keep yourselves from being *aware* of your anger. But don't be misled, these mental games may keep you from *recognizing* your anger, but they don't keep you from *being* angry deep inside yourself.

A second misunderstanding is closely related. You might express it this way: "I can't keep from getting angry, but I can keep others from knowing about it." This attitude is related to the "being nice" idea we discussed earlier. If you function this way, you use a lot of energy trying to hide your anger from your parents, your spouse, your children, your fellow workers, and others to whom you relate. In fact, the anger which you try not to show is probably creating problems for you—which we will describe in Chapter 4.

Behind this misunderstanding is the assumption that good Christians do not show their anger. You may have believed that the most ethical way to live, the most loving way to relate to others, is to keep anger out of your relationships. Therefore, each time you are successful in keeping your anger secret, you feel that you are following God's will. This belief ignores the warning of both Jesus and Paul that hiding our anger is dangerous. We will see later that Christians have a responsibility for handling anger in a more honest and creative manner.

Chapter 2
What Is Anger?

You and I must take a new look at the questions: "Where does anger come from?" and "Why do people get angry?" Since these questions have intrigued many psychologists and sociologists, our answer must take seriously what these authorities have learned about anger from their research. We must also reexamine our Christian heritage for more understanding and guidance concerning our experiences with anger.

Most interpretations and explanations of anger given by social scientists have one common feature—*anger occurs when you, or those important to you, are threatened.* In the next few pages you and I will explore this basic truth and develop a new understanding of anger.

WHY DO YOU GET ANGRY?

What causes you to get angry? A threat to your selfhood! When anger occurs, two things are present: a person and a threat. When you feel anger, you feel threatened or endangered by something. What happens to you when you hear a crashing noise downstairs in the middle of the night, or realize that your daughter is an hour late returning home from a blind date, or hear someone laughing *at* you, or see that your son has failed to do his chores *again,* or hear a speech ridiculing an idea you believe to be true? What happens when you sense

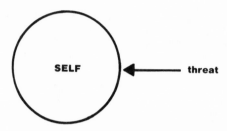

yourself (or those people, ideas, and things which are important to you) to be in danger? You feel anxious!

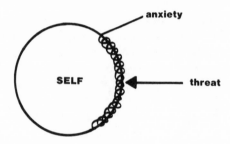

Any threat to your selfhood triggers an internal alarm system indicating that you are under attack. Whether you want to or not, your whole being goes on alert, mobilizing in response to the threatening situation.

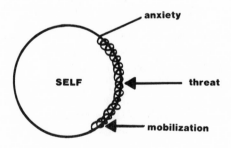

In such situations, you are probably aware of changes in your body, which include rising blood pressure, rapid heartbeat, tensed muscles, and increased perspiration. Chemicals that make you tense and alert, such as adrenalin, are pumped into your bloodstream. Your body is getting primed to fight or run away. Nature is preparing you to defend yourself or to escape the danger.

This response in your body is basic, but you also mobilize mentally. Have you noticed how you become more alert, your awareness is heightened, and your mind tries to figure out what you should do in the face of this threat? You consider various possibilities and plan how to protect yourself.

For our purposes, however, the emotions that get aroused are the most important part of this mobilizing response. The anxiety, which you feel when alarmed, produces two emotional reactions: fear and *anger.*

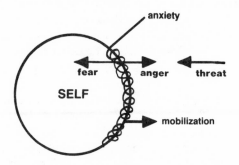

These emotions are obvious when we are responding to a threat.

> Several nights ago, my wife and I were driving downtown on the interstate highway. Suddenly a truck on my right began moving into my lane to make a left turn ahead. I slammed on the brakes and cut to the left shoulder, trying to avoid both a ditch and a bridge support just ahead! I barely missed both truck and bridge! You can

imagine my panic! My heart was pumping furiously, my stomach was tied in knots, and I broke out in a cold sweat. Within those split seconds I felt both fear and anger: fear of injury, pain, and suffering, and anger toward the driver for either careless driving or deliberately risking an accident. (Of course, he may not have seen us and might have been innocent of malicious intent, but when I felt threatened, my first response was to assume that the attack was premeditated!) In a few seconds I was safe, but it took a while before my body returned to normal, and the fear and anger subsided.

You have been in similar situations. If you take a moment to recall your response, you will be able to remember the fear and anger present in the anxiety which occurs when you (or anyone else) are threatened.

In summary, when you are threatened, you automatically become anxious. Anxiety is a word that describes the physical, mental, and emotional "call to arms" that enables people to defend or escape a perceived danger. The emotions you feel within this anxiety include fear and anger. When angry, you can be sure that you are anxious. The fact that you are anxious is a signal that you think you are in danger or threatened in some way.

The amount of fear and anger you feel will be determined by how big the threat seems. If it appears small, your anger will not be very strong. If you think the threat is dangerous, then your anger will be more intense. Of course something that seems to be a big threat to one person may present little or no threat to another.

Notice that you may not recognize right away the anger within anxiety. Your fear may be so strong, or the need to escape so immediate, that your anger does not appear until later. Another common reason, as I have mentioned, is that your social and religious training either keeps you from being aware of the anger or causes you to hide it. When you or I do not acknowledge anger, many problems result for us and for those with whom we live and work. We will address these problems in a later chapter.

WHAT THREATENS YOU?

I am using the word *threat* to represent people, ideas, events, or situations that you consider to be dangerous. It would be easy to underestimate the many different ways in which you can be threatened, so I need to describe three aspects of your selfhood which are vulnerable—life and health, relationships, and self-esteem.

THREATS TO THE PHYSICAL SELF

The most obvious and immediate aspect of your self is the physical body in which you are packaged! If your body is endangered, you automatically feel threatened → which brings out anxiety → which expresses itself with anger. Why do you and I get angry with reckless drivers, burglars, cancer, pollution, a doctor who missed an important diagnosis, and so forth? Because each is a threat to our physical well-being. Our health (therefore our life) is in jeopardy.

> Janey and I were talking as she waited to enter the hospital for exploratory surgery to discover the source of cancerous cells. The doctors hoped to find a self-contained malignancy in her uterus, but it was possible that the cancer had spread to, or come from, some other part of the body. Janey was describing her anxiety, talking about her fear of death and leaving her husband and mother. But she was also very aware of her anger and quite concerned about taking it out on the children she taught. "Those poor kids don't deserve it, but I've been a real bitch! You wouldn't believe how fussy and irritable I've been."

People who work with sick patients and their families in hospitals know that such fear and anger lie just below the surface. Some tension is always present because disease and illness are threats to human life. You or I or anybody would become anxious. Our anger is controlled most of the time, both by the predominance of fear and by social custom. But this anger over a threat to health often "leaks out" (from both patients and families) onto doctors, nurses, visitors, hospital policy, or even the food service!

THREATS TO THE SOCIAL SELF

People are not only identified with their bodies but also with social relationships. You are a social creature and therefore dependent on relationships for security and meaning. Your network of family and friends is a significant aspect of your self. The need to love and to be loved is powerful. Therefore, when any of your relationships are in danger, you experience anxiety and feel angry at the threat.

> Barbara called late one night saying she and her husband, Don, had a major problem and needed to see me quickly. Barbara had confessed an affair in which she had been involved for six months. The immediate problem was Don's anger, which was expressed in several forms—disillusionment, hurt, and rage being the most important. His first reaction was to "throw her out on the street." Later his anger focused on the other man. As Don worked through his emotions he could easily imagine physically "beating up this other man" or at least "exposing the affair at his workplace so that the man would have to resign."

For Don to be angry is not surprising, but to understand him within our present framework might be helpful. Don received much of his meaning in life from his family. He valued marriage and invested a good portion of his identity in being a stable family man. Now this part of his selfhood was in jeopardy. At first his wife's behavior was perceived as the threat, and most of his anger was directed toward her. Then his focus changed and the other man became the threat. Don supposed that the other man had "taken advantage" of Barbara's weaknesses. His anger was then concentrated on this intruder.

Sexual infidelity is not the only threat to a marriage relationship. Most spouses expect to be treated as special, to be given first place by their partner. They also expect to meet their needs for togetherness, companionship, and affection within the relationship. Therefore, if the partner seems to be more committed to work, study, or hobby than to the marriage, the spouse becomes threatened → anxious → angry.

> Jim began driving his stockcar at a local racetrack. When his team began doing well, Jim started traveling on weekends to tracks in a four-state area. During the week the men worked on the car at night, so that Jim often spent the night at the garage. Sue became angry at racing, finally at Jim. He never understood why she was upset with something he enjoyed so much. She said: "He loves the car more than he loves me! He sleeps with it more than with me!" They finally separated and she divorced him.

Sue needed affirmation from Jim. She wanted to feel important to him, receive and give affection, and spend time with him and their little girl. Racing, the car, and Jim's commitment to it threatened a relationship that was very significant to her. She spent several years being anxious and fearful that racing would end her marriage. Finally the anger, which was part of the anxiety, became her dominant emotion. This anger motivated her to reduce the threat of being unloved by leaving to look for another relationship.

THREATS TO SELF-ESTEEM

You have a personal identity which includes a body and relationships, but is more comprehensive. Personal identity includes an internal sense of self. This aspect of selfhood includes how you feel about yourself, often called self-esteem. Your self-esteem includes your personal value system and moral commitments (self-integrity), and what you wish you were or think you ought to be (ideal self). When your self-esteem takes a blow, when you violate your integrity, or when you fall way short of your ideals, you feel threatened. Your anxiety expresses itself through anger.

You may not like to think so, but an important part of your self-esteem is related to the way you imagine other people think about you. You want to be liked, respected, popular, trusted, admired, and so forth. When something happens that affirms you, such as getting a promotion, or a pay raise, being elected to an office, having flowers sent by your spouse, or an unexpected kiss from your child, then your self-esteem soars. On the other hand, self-esteem can be damaged by a failure, an embarrassment, criticism, making a mistake, being left out, getting laughed at or ridiculed. When such events take place you become very conscious of the anxiety that sweeps over you. You are threatened because your self-esteem is being lowered by another person's judgment.

> Ana angrily related that two weeks earlier a nephew of her husband had called to ask her and her husband, Rich, if they would consider being godparents for the nephew's new baby. Ana was pleased with the possibility. However, another relative called with the news that the nephew was going to ask Rich to be the godfather, but would not be asking Ana to be the godmother. Ana was furious. She "stomped down the stairs" angrily denouncing these in-laws for their "insensitivity, prejudice, and religious bias." She had shouted at her husband and warned him that she would consider him "stupid" if he agreed to the nephew's request.

Ana was experienced in using the ideas you and I are exploring in this chapter. When I asked about her experience and she tried to understand her anger, she was quick to recognize the threat to her self-esteem. She always considers herself as being in the shadow of her husband, a lawyer/politician who is outgoing and well liked. Like any person, she wants to be recognized in her own right. She had been working for many months to accept herself and reduce her dependence on other people's opinions. This blatant rejection, however, was a serious threat to her self-esteem. Ana's heated response was the defensive anger generated in the face of this threat.

You and I have seen how your self can be threatened by the actions of others. Now we must explore how you can be threatened by your own actions! Self-integrity is a major ingredient of self-esteem. You might call it the conscience. Your conscience is that inner sense of right and wrong, good and bad which you have developed over the years. It is rooted in what you learned as a child from family, school, and church. Value systems you have adopted in adulthood and moral commitments you have chosen are also a part of this self-integrity. Personal integrity is an important aspect of your self. Obviously, when you act or fail to act in a way that violates your conscience, you feel threatened. This threat provokes a type of anxiety we call *guilt.* Within this anxiety (guilt), of course, is anger.

You may be able to express the anger toward yourself for whatever created the threat. This would be an appropriate way to hold yourself accountable for breaking your moral commitment. Being genuinely angry with yourself can lead to confession, repentance, and the experience of forgiveness. However, in the face of a threat it is easy to blame someone else or the circumstances. This is one way people try to protect themselves from the anxiety of guilt experienced when moral commitments are violated.

You are also threatened when you fall short of your "ideal self." As you grew up you learned from family, church, and society what characterizes the "best" people. You learned how good little boys and girls, sons and daughters should behave. Later you were taught how good parents function and how ideal wives and husbands respond to each other. If you grew up in the church, you were taught various ideas about what good Christians should do and be. All along, these lessons were shaping your ideals. In some corner of your mind an ideal self developed that represented what kind of person you wished to become. This ideal self mirrors your secret hopes of being perfect.

I would not deny that the ideal self is an important motivating force. It pulls and pushes you to attain your goals and fulfill your potential. However, it also becomes a source of threat. In actual life your *ideal* self and your *real* self are two different things. You are painfully aware that you do not measure up to your ideal self. When some event reminds you of your failure to be what you want to be, your self is threatened. There results a type of anxiety called *shame,* which, of course, also contains anger. The more unrealistic a person's ideal self,

the more likely that he or she will fall short and feel angry.

You probably know firsthand how these various threats to self-esteem (self-integrity and the ideal self) overlap and get mixed together in day-to-day living. Let me give you an example of the vicious circle which can develop when the anger generated by one threat becomes itself the next threat.

> Sharon, a mother of two boys, four and two years old, came for counseling because "I'm depressed all the time" and "worrying about whether I'm a good mother or not." These feelings were related to the intense anger she had been expressing toward her little boys. Sharon had been brought up "to behave" by expressing no negative emotions. She had admired the calm, cool way in which her mother kept house and entertained. Now, as the mother of two rambunctious, curious, active boys, she was unable to keep house the way she had imagined (ideal self) she would. Therefore, when the boys "messed things up," her ideal self as a housekeeper was threatened and she would get angry. Her ideal self also demanded that she, as a "good" mother, would have "good" children. "Good" meant quiet, neat, and helpful, like she had been as a child. When her sons were noisy, messy, and uninterested in helping, her ideal of herself as a mother was threatened. Furthermore, as the younger boy began walking and causing more commotion, her anger increased. She felt she was abusing them by "tongue-lashing" them and "spanking them too hard," which made her feel guilty.

Sharon's self-esteem was besieged on three sides because she was unable to match her ideal self as a housekeeper, as an effective mother who could raise "good" children, or as a person who always stayed calm and never got angry.

The final stage of these problems, which finally brought Sharon to the counseling center, was depression. The increased anxiety that she felt when she "abused" her sons produced more intense anger. But instead of expressing it toward the boys, her fear of abusing them and her growing sense of worthlessness made her turn the anger in on herself in depression. I will describe how anger is related to depression in a later chapter.

THE EXTENDED SELF

To complete this understanding of anger, I must call attention to the *self* which gets threatened. It is important for you to grasp the scope of your personhood and identify the many ways you have extended your self. Like other people, you do not exist in isolation. You have involved yourself with other people, things, and ideas. When other people, groups, beliefs, or values to which you are attached become threatened, then *you* become threatened → anxious → and angry on their behalf.

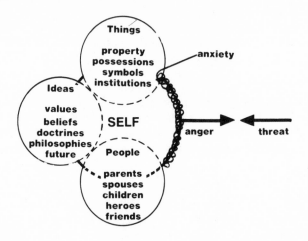

PEOPLE

The most obvious investment you make of yourself is with other people. I mentioned earlier the importance of community and the impact of threats to relationships. If some event or person threatens your spouse, your parents, one of your children, a friend, or one of your heroes, then *you* feel threatened. These people have become part of you and you don't want anybody hurting them.

Furthermore, you are invested not only in individuals but also in groups, such as your social club, your business, your church, and your bowling team. You don't like it when they are attacked or ridiculed.

> My thirteen-year-old son is a loyal sports fan of our state university. He hangs team pictures on his walls, wears shirts and hats with team symbols, and collects autographs from the players. He strongly identifies himself with their excellent basketball team. Anything that threatens their championship dreams, such as opposing teams, critical sports announcers, and referees, also makes my son feel personally threatened. He gets anxious on their behalf and expresses the aroused anger loudly (particularly at the referees).

IDEAS AND VALUES

You also get invested in ideas. Your community values, religious doctrines, belief systems, and philosophies become a significant part of your selfhood. You have become identified with them—they are "yours." Therefore, if ideas important to you are threatened by others (disregarded, ridiculed, made legal or illegal, disagreed with), *you* become threatened → which creates anxiety → which includes the emotional response of anger.

> My son and I were playing a board game on the floor in his room. Denise, my nine-year-old daughter, came in to watch. She tried to talk with us but we were deep in the game. She reached out and moved one of Scott's pieces. He politely asked her not to touch anything. A few minutes later she again reached out and disturbed some of the pieces. This time Scott was annoyed and

more forcefully told her to "leave it alone!" This second time I also became irritated. When Denise stretched out the third time to tinker with something on the board, my irritation instantly switched to anger. Within a split second I had "spanked" her hand! (Later she called it a "slap," which I must admit was more accurate.) Her hand and her feelings were hurt, and she left for her room in tears.

I had responded angrily, but why? My life was not in danger, my community was not under fire, nor was my self-esteem being directly attacked. It was obvious that I had been threatened, however, or I would not have gotten so furious. On reflection, I could recognize that several of my values had been threatened. I place a high value on listening to other people and taking what they say seriously. I also value respecting other people's "territory." Denise had contradicted these two values. It is also part of my ideal self that my children would adopt and live out my value system. That my own daughter was, at that moment, not being thoughtful and sensitive was also threatening.

Current debates over abortion, prayer in the classroom, and whether creationism should be taught beside evolution in the schools have sparked anger on both sides. These controversies demonstrate the amount of threat which people feel when their belief systems are under attack.

THE FUTURE

You have also extended yourself by investing in your future. Dreaming is one of the privileges of being human. God has given us the capacity to anticipate and plan the future. Your dreams have become part of you. If some person or event threatens your future, you will feel threatened and angry.

Janet, partially paralyzed from multiple sclerosis, was visibly upset and angry when we talked. Her physical therapist had told her that further work in the rehabilitation unit would not be helpful. Janet was aware that she had not been making progress recently, but had tried to ignore this disturbing fact. To hear the expert say that no more could be done was quite a shock. As we talked, Janet expressed her anger toward the therapist for giving her the bad news before Christmas. She was also terribly angry at what she calls her "disease process." Why this anger? Let me share more of the story.

Several years ago while caring for a dying mother, Janet began to imagine becoming a chaplain in a hospital. The dream developed into a sense of call as she made plans to attend seminary. As she was beginning her studies she became ill with multiple sclerosis. In the last four years she has suffered through several major attacks, the most recent leaving her paralyzed except for her right arm and her head. She made amazing recovery from this attack and, at a rehabilitation center, learned to use what mobility she did have to take care of herself and live independently. During this ordeal she has never lost sight of her goal of being a minister in a hospital. Now, however, there had been no further progress in physical therapy.

Why had Janet been so angry in our last conversation? Her future was threatened. She had continued hoping that she would learn to walk again, assuming she would need to walk to be a chaplain. Now her dream was shattered and she was threatened, anxious, and angry. Objectively speaking, Janet may still be able to serve as a chaplain in a motorized wheelchair. However, from her perspective the future was being changed by her disease. She was appropriately threatened and angry.

THINGS AND PLACES

People get attached to different possessions, such as homes, cars, heirlooms, furniture, and pets (they are not things, of course, but not human either, so I include them here). You and I invest things with meaning and develop relationships with them. Certain belongings become very important to us and symbolize something significant to our selfhood. If they are threatened, we get threatened → anxious → angry.

This is one reason why children get angry when one of their favorite toys breaks. You have seen people get angry over dents in their cars, baseballs in their flower gardens, and spills on their rugs.

> My friend Linda came home to find the house burgla-rized and ransacked. She was threatened by the invasion of privacy, but felt the most anger toward the intruders for stealing jewelry that had been given to her by her mother and husband, now deceased.

UNDERSTANDING ANGER

I hope this discussion of "Why do people get angry?" and "Where does anger come from?" will be helpful as you try to understand your own anger. Remember—when you are angry, it means that something has threatened your selfhood (including those people, ideas, values, and things that are significant to you). The threat may be physical, social, or psychological. It may come from an event, a group, another person, or from differing values and beliefs.

When you are threatened, you have a natural, God-given response—you get anxious. One of the emotional parts of this anxiety is the anger that you feel. A helpful way to understand a particular experience of anger is to follow this process of evaluation. (1) I am angry, therefore I must be anxious. (2) If I am anxious, something has threatened me or something important to me. (3) What is this threat? This chapter gives you plenty of questions to ask that will help you identify the threat. This process can also be used to understand the anger of other people. When other people (family, friends) are angry, that means they are threatened → anxious → angry. When the threats are recognized, you can take responsibility for dealing

with your anger (and perhaps the anger of others) more creatively and ethically. We will return to the question of how
Christians should handle their anger in the last chapter.

An important conclusion from this explanation of anger
must be noted. *All human beings get angry!* As we saw in the
previous chapter, there are those in the Christian tradition who
believe that they should never get angry. However, as we have
seen in this discussion of anger, it is not possible to keep from
experiencing anger. All human beings get threatened at some
time, in some way, by some situations. In the next chapter we
will discover that the Bible reveals this same truth about
human nature, and in Chapter 6 we will discuss more theological reasons why all human beings get threatened. In fact, as we
shall see in Chapter 5, Christians *should* be threatened by some
situations (injustice, for example) and get angry in response.

Chapter 3
What Does the Bible Say?

The Bible is certainly a book about God. However, it also deals with God's creation, particularly that part of the creation called human beings (like you and me). In its pages we find revelation not only about who God is but about who we are. Since Scripture is a frank account of human life, we should not be surprised to find many descriptions of anger in the lives of its characters. Indeed, the Bible has much to say about anger.

Sadly, much of what Scripture does say about anger is either ignored or misinterpreted because of prejudices already established. For example, if you are a Christian who has been taught to think that anger is always bad, you probably read Scripture through glasses already colored by that religious belief. You may assume that Scripture supports the view that "good" Christians should not *show* anger and that the "best" Christians will not even *feel* angry. As we examine some of the biblical messages about anger we will find that these assumptions are not correct.

We will see that the Bible takes for granted that anger is part of human nature, part of how God created us. It is also clear that anger can lead to sin, and both Old and New Testaments criticize destructive expressions of anger. We will see, however, that when Scripture disapproves of an angry event, it is passing judgment on the *results* of mishandled anger rather than on the *experience* of anger.

THE OLD TESTAMENT

We will find our first example at the very beginning of the Bible within one of the oldest stories in our heritage.

CAIN'S SIN

The Genesis story about Abel's murder at the hands of his brother, Cain, is one of the earliest stories of anger in human relationships. Cain's experience is instructive. It is easy for people to make the assumption: "Anger led Cain to kill his brother, so anger is bad. Therefore, to be angry is to sin." But read the story again.

> In the course of time Cain brought to the LORD an offering of the fruit of the ground, and Abel brought of the firstlings of his flock and of their fat portions. And the LORD had regard for Abel and his offering, but for Cain and his offering he had no regard. So Cain was very angry, and his countenance fell. The LORD said to Cain, "Why are you angry, and why has your countenance fallen? If you do well, will you not be accepted? And if you do not do well, sin is couching at the door; its desire is for you, but you must master it." (Gen. 4:3–7)

As this story passed from generation to generation and finally into written form, the reason why Cain's offering was not accepted has been lost. Clearly Cain's response was to be "very angry." Perhaps the Lord's words, "If you do well, will you not be accepted?" indicate that Cain had not followed instructions or had not been faithful to some ritual. If so, Cain's anger may have been his response to the threat he felt from guilt and/or shame. Or maybe Cain's anger was related to his loss of self-esteem because he felt rejected. In any case, Cain was threatened by the event → became anxious → and felt angry.

For our purposes it is important to realize that even though Cain "was very angry," he was not accused of sinning. Did the

Lord say, "You have no right to be angry" or "You have sinned against me because you are angry"? No! Instead, God pointed out to Cain that because he was angry he was more exposed to temptation. God warned him that "sin is couching at the door; its desire is for you." Anger can work in the service of evil, but it doesn't have to! Cain could choose to sin with his anger (which, in fact, he did) but he could have chosen to use the anger creatively for spiritual growth. The Lord said he had the opportunity and the responsibility to "master" the anger. We will talk about anger as a positive force in Chapter 5 and how to handle anger in Chapter 7.

THE WISDOM SAYINGS

The Hebrews of long ago expressed their ideas about human nature in the wisdom sayings, some of which are recorded in Proverbs and Ecclesiastes. Their thoughts about anger are sometimes distorted by Christians. For example, if asked the question, "What does the book of Proverbs say about anger?" many church members would answer, "A wise person doesn't get angry." Not so! The wisdom sayings do not describe godly persons as those who never get angry. Examine for yourself the following passages from the Hebrew Wisdom Literature.

> A man of quick temper acts foolishly,
>   but a man of discretion is patient.
>   (Prov. 14:17)

> He who is slow to anger has great understanding,
>   but he who has a hasty temper exalts folly.
>   (Prov. 14:29)

> He who is slow to anger is better than the
>   mighty, and he who rules his spirit than he who
>   takes a city.
>   (Prov. 16:32)

> Good sense makes a man slow to anger, and it is his
>   glory to overlook an offense.
>
> (Prov. 19:11)

> Be not quick to anger, for anger lodges in
>   the bosom of fools.
>
> (Eccl. 7:9)

You do not have to be a Bible scholar to realize that these verses are describing godly persons as those persons *who are careful* with their anger. The Hebrews knew that the emotion of anger is part of human nature as created by God. Hebrew Wisdom Literature does not paint a picture of humans who never feel any anger. Instead, it challenges God's people to take ethical responsibility for evaluating *what* to get angry at and *how* to express the anger that they *do* experience. These wisdom sayings are concerned about temper tantrums and explosive hostility. Anger that is separated from our capacity to think is perceived as immature. Anger that boils over becomes problem-causing rather than problem-solving.

JESUS AND ANGER

As a Christian who seeks to understand the place and meaning of anger in human experience, you will want to examine closely the life, work, and words of Jesus.

JESUS: A HUMAN BEING WITH EMOTIONS

You may find it hard to accept the "humanness" of the carpenter from Nazareth. Despite the careful attempts of church councils and denominational creeds to balance the divinity and the humanity of Jesus, your Christian upbringing may have emphasized the divinity of Jesus (the Son of God) and discounted the humanness of Jesus (the Son of Man). If you also learned that God doesn't have emotions, the result is the idea that Jesus had no feelings. Of course, people who hold such a view would agree that Jesus loves, but they describe love as a nice, thoughtful character trait rather empty of actual passion.

A closer look at the Gospels gives a different, and more realistic, picture. The Gospel writers tell us that Jesus felt the full range of human emotion—sorrow, frustration, fear, grief, irritation, disappointment, indignation, and anger. God's incarnation was complete. Jesus was fully human and took part in every aspect of humanness, including anxiety in the face of threats to his selfhood.

When Jesus went into Gethsemane to pray, for example, he was obviously aware of the coming confrontation with the Pharisees and the possibility of being arrested, convicted, and executed. As you would expect of any person, Jesus was threatened by the possibility of death and the failure of his mission. The anxiety which this threat created within Jesus is openly described by the Gospel writers. Matthew says he was "sorrowful and troubled" (Matt. 26:37). Mark notes that he was "greatly distressed" (Mark 14:33). Luke describes him in such "agony" that "his sweat became like great drops of blood falling upon the ground" (Luke 22:44). Who among us has not felt this kind of anxiety?

We have learned that fear and anger are normal emotional responses when persons are anxious in the face of threats. The man from Galilee was no exception. Fear is present in his request of the Father, "Remove this cup from me" (Mark 14:36). Can you hear the anger expressed when Jesus returns to his disciples and finds them asleep—"Simon, are you asleep? Could you not watch one hour?" (V. 37). Later, on the cross, the fear and anger are disclosed again when Jesus cries out, "My God, my God, why hast thou forsaken me?" (Mark 15:34).

WHEN JESUS GOT ANGRY

Does it shock you to think of Jesus the Christ getting anxious and being angry? Do you wonder whether Jesus was *that* human? Well, let's look at some other events recorded in the

Gospels. Read again the story about Jesus cleansing the Temple. All four Gospels record this event, but we will use John's description.

> The Passover of the Jews was at hand, and Jesus went up to Jerusalem. In the temple he found those who were selling oxen and sheep and pigeons, and the money-changers at their business. And making a whip of cords, he drove them all, with the sheep and oxen, out of the temple; and he poured out the coins of the money-changers and overturned their tables. And he told those who sold the pigeons, "Take these things away; you shall not make my Father's house a house of trade." (John 2: 13–16)

Can you picture this wild scene? A chaotic few minutes burned into the disciples' minds. One passionate rabbi with a whip of cords suddenly moving against the establishment and driving them from the courtyard. Tables overturn with a crash, pigeons flutter loose, oxen bray, sheep bleat, coins clang and roll around the floor, animals scatter, people shout and dodge the whip, shocked gasps (and maybe some cheers!) escape from the stunned crowd. Whether or not Jesus hit anyone, we must realize the explosiveness of his action. These established rip-off artists would not have been intimidated and scattered easily. They were moved by the fury of his words, and the obvious strength of his physical presence. The disciples, amazed at his intensity, were reminded of the psalmist who wrote, "Zeal for thy house will consume me" (John 2:17).

Could anyone read this account and doubt that Jesus was angry? Why should it surprise us that Jesus would be indignant at injustice? The money-changers were making a mockery of worship, were insulting God, and were profiting from Jewish law. The Bible often pictures God's wrath in the face of human injustice. Jesus acted in a prophetic way. But many who read of this event in the life of Jesus are shocked. Arthur Gossip says of this passage,

Desperate attempts have been made by some who feel uncomfortable over it to tone it down and edge out this incident . . . because they feel unhappily that it will not fit into their preconceived idea of what Christ should do and be; that here somehow he acted for once out of character, and fell inexplicably below himself, forgot his own law of life, lost his head and his temper. (*The Interpreter's Bible,* Vol. 8, pp. 497–498)

You may have had your own doubts about this passage. If you have believed all your life that Christians should not allow themselves to feel anger (or express it if they do), then you will certainly try to explain this event in some other way.

To take the event as it stands, however, allows us to learn something important. Jesus, like all humans, got angry. However, he did not sin with his anger! His anger was mobilized in the service of love as he protested superficial religion and acted out God's displeasure. If we could accept that Jesus was angry, maybe we could accept our own anger and take more ethical responsibility for our emotional responses.

JESUS AND THE PHARISEES

Scripture also reports that Jesus was angry when he confronted the Pharisees concerning whether or not it was appropriate to heal on the Sabbath.

Again he entered the synagogue, and a man was there who had a withered hand. And they watched him, to see whether he would heal him on the sabbath, so that they might accuse him. And he said to the man who had the withered hand, "Come here." And he said to them, "Is it lawful on the sabbath to do good or to do harm, to save life or to kill?" But they were silent. And he looked around at them with anger, grieved at their hardness of heart, and said to the man, "Stretch out your hand." He stretched it out, and his hand was restored. (Mark 3:1–5)

No question here about what was going on inside Jesus as he looked around at the Pharisees. When Mark describes what emotion Jesus was feeling, he uses the Greek word *orge*—the word for anger most commonly used in the New Testament. It cannot be translated any other way than *anger!*

If you believe that being angry in any way, at any time, about anything, is to be sinful, Mark's report puts you in a dilemma! Why? Traditionally, Christians believe that (1) Jesus was able to live out his life in obedience to the will of God (he was "without sin") and also that (2) the Bible is a trustworthy account of the life and work of Jesus. Do you agree with these statements? If so, then you cannot logically believe that being angry is always a sin! Why not? Because, if you insist that feeling angry is sinful, but also believe that Jesus was without sin, then you have to throw out Mark's Gospel, because it clearly testifies that Jesus got angry. You can't afford to believe that Jesus got angry or you would have to label him a sinner.

On the other hand, if you consider Mark's eyewitness account of Jesus to be accurate, yet continue to hold on to the notion that being angry is sinful, then you must conclude that Jesus sinned when he got angry. Now you have to give up the idea that Jesus was sinless. Do you see what problems are caused when you equate anger with sin? I hope you keep your belief in the trustworthiness of the Bible and the perfect obedience of Jesus the Christ. Then you can give up the idea that to experience the emotion of anger automatically means that you have sinned.

As you read the Gospels, notice the other times when Jesus was angry. He was frustrated when the disciples tried to keep parents from bringing children into his presence (Mark 10: 13–14). He was indignant when he told Herod's messenger, "Go and tell that fox . . . " (Luke 13:32) and angry when he called the Pharisees "whitewashed tombs" and "serpents" (Matt. 23:27, 33). Even the disciple Peter caught an angry response when Jesus rebuked him with the words, "Get behind me, Satan" (Matt. 16:23).

"SHALL BE LIABLE TO JUDGMENT"

The biblical passage most often quoted by those who defend the position that "Christians shouldn't get angry" is the following from the Sermon on the Mount.

> You have heard that it was said to the men of old, "You shall not kill; and whoever kills shall be liable to the judgment." But I say to you that every one who is angry with his brother shall be liable to judgment; whoever insults his brother shall be liable to the council, and whoever says, "You fool!" shall be liable to the hell of fire. (Matt. 5:21–22)

When you first read this passage it sounds as if any feeling of anger is the same as committing murder. Indeed, this verse has been used throughout Christian history to make people think that any experience of anger is the same in God's sight as killing someone. Closer examination of the Greek text, however, reveals a more accurate understanding. The verb *orgizesthai,* translated "is angry," is a present participle and refers to continuous action. A more exact translation would be "everyone who is *continuously* angry" or "everyone who *keeps on being* angry." Many translators are more exact than the Revised Standard Version quoted above. Charles Williams translates this phrase, "everyone who harbors malice against his brother," and the New English Bible reads, "anyone who nurses anger against his brother."

So, you can see that Jesus is not talking about every experience of anger. Many Christians respond to this passage as if Jesus had said, "If you ever have the slightest feeling of anger in your heart, you are a terrible person and will be judged harshly!" But this is not what Jesus was concerned about. He *is* concerned about anger that lies unresolved in the heart, festering until it bursts forth in destructive behavior—such as insulting others (v. 22) and calling them fools (v. 22). Like the authors of Proverbs, Jesus points out that anger nursed and fertilized in the inner self becomes destructive of human personality and is as distasteful to God as is murder. If we allow anger to simmer demonically inside us, it will poison our interpersonal relationships. Perhaps this is why Jesus follows his statement about anger with an admonition to work toward reconciliation of conflicts (vs. 23–25). When our anger is allowed to destroy individuals and alienate relationships, we certainly deserve judgment, but this does not mean that every time we get angry we have sinned.

If you memorized the passage under discussion from the King James Version, you will remember the phrase "without a cause." You may recall hearing a person excuse some destructive form of anger (such as revenge, jealousy, or a long-standing resentment) because somebody had given them "cause" (a reason to be that way). But the oldest manuscripts of the Bible do not include this phrase and present-day translations of the Bible include it only in the margins. I have often wondered if this phrase was added by a scribe who knew personally that all people get angry and wanted to provide some escape from the seemingly harsh words of Jesus. However, recognizing the true meaning of the verb allows us to realize that Jesus was calling attention to the devastating results of unreconciled anger, not the experience of anger itself.

THE EPHESIAN LETTER

Ephesians expresses the maturing faith of the early church as it confronts the Gentile world. The fourth chapter exhorts Christians "to lead a life worthy of the calling" to be God's people (v. 1), stressing the unity of the church (vs. 3–6) and the necessity of integrating different gifts (v. 11) for the growth and maturation of each Christian (vs. 12–16). Individual Christians are challenged to "grow up . . . into Christ" (v. 15) by living differently from those "alienated from the life of God" (vs. 17–18). We must put away the corrupt "old nature" and "put on the new nature, created after the likeness of God" (vs. 22–24).

After this magnificent challenge, Paul begins to give specific guidance on how those in Christ should be different. He begins with a significant, but often overlooked, passage.

> Therefore, putting away falsehood, let every one speak the truth with his neighbor, for we are members one of another. Be angry but do not sin; do not let the sun go down on your anger, and give no opportunity to the devil. (Eph. 4:25–27)

Interestingly, the first concern is for honest communication. I will return to the relationship of Christian candor to anger in a few pages, but first we will study Paul's ideas about anger. He quotes from Ps. 4:4 when he writes, "Be angry but do not sin." What? Is he telling the church to get angry? No, the Greek is more accurately translated "If you are angry" (New English Bible) or "When angry, do not sin" (The Amplified New Testament). Paul recognizes, indeed assumes, that Christians (like all human beings) with their different backgrounds, values, and personalities were bound to find themselves angry with each other.

Throughout church history, some Christians have acted as if Paul said, "Don't you dare allow yourselves to get angry, that would be sinful!" As you can see, however, Paul makes no judgment on the fact that Christians *experience* anger. He is concerned about what we *do* with our anger. The point of these verses is to admonish Christians not to sin when they are angry. The New English Bible translates it "do not let anger lead you into sin."

How can you sin with your anger? The wise author of Ephesians knows that if you try to ignore your anger and pretend that you are not feeling it, then you become more likely to sin with your anger. In fact, a few verses later (v. 31), Paul describes some of the destructive offspring of unresolved anger, namely, "bitterness," "slander," and "malice." So Paul warns Christians to take care of their anger promptly, today, before the sun goes down.

The apostle adds a further perception about the importance of being responsible with our anger. He points out that to let anger go unresolved is to "give opportunity to the devil." Allowing anger to go unattended is to ignore its potential harmfulness and to join hands with the destructive forces in life, but more about that in Chapter 4.

Was it accidental that the injunction "Be angry but do not sin" comes immediately after the command to put away falsehood? I think not. Misrepresenting reality, distorting facts, using language to cover up instead of to reveal is dishonest. The mature Christian "puts away falsehood" and "speaks the truth" with others as a way of life.

This concern for forthrightness in speech is found at other points in the New Testament. When Jesus speaks out against swearing in the Sermon on the Mount, he suggests "Let what you say be simply 'Yes' or 'No'; anything more than this comes from evil" (Matt. 5:37). Directness of speech is also called for in James: "But let your yes be yes and your no be no, that you may not fall under condemnation" (James 5:12).

The author is not only thinking of the need to contain explosive anger which causes violence and open conflict. His concern that anger be handled *today* (before the sun goes down) would reflect his awareness of damage done to the church by those who ignore their anger or pretend they are not angry. These people, because of fear or false notions of what it means to be nice, work overtime to hide their anger from others. In fact, however, they are falsifying reality and are sinning against their brothers and sisters by communicating a lie!

CONCLUSION

You can see that from the Bible's point of view anger is a normal part of human nature. The potential to feel angry is rooted in God's created order. In fact, if the Bible makes it clear that God gets angry, and if we are created in God's image, it makes sense that we would have the same potential for anger. We have seen that Jesus became angry.

The Bible also recognizes that people sin with their anger. No one is excused for expressing anger in destructive ways. Yes, you and I sin with our anger, but that does not mean we have sinned every time we feel this emotion. To *feel* anger is not the same as sinning *with* it. It is what we *do* with our anger that raises the moral questions of good and evil. In the next chapter we will examine the destructive ways in which anger is handled.

Chapter 4
Anger Can Be Destructive

It should be clear by now that anger is a normal part of human existence. It is a planned and important feature of the created order. If we did not feel anxiety, along with the emotional responses of fear and anger, we human beings would not have survived. Anger motivates action and behavior that protects us by enabling us to escape danger and defend against attacks on our selfhood. It is obvious that anger is a necessary and potentially good part of our basic nature. In fact, the next chapter will discuss how anger can be a helpful contributor to a mature Christian life. But in this chapter we must examine the dark side of anger.

Unfortunately, anger not only has a positive function, but, like most other things in life, it can be distorted and misused. Anger can become a vehicle of destruction. We are most aware of anger expressed violently (rape, spouse and child abuse, muggings, murder) or explosively (yelling, swearing, driving recklessly, slamming doors, temper tantrums). You know how it hurts when you are the victim of such anger. Most of us, when we are honest, will admit to having displayed our anger in such outbursts. We know firsthand the disastrous effect on our relationships with family and friends.

However, I am constantly aware of the hurt and anguish caused by anger that is *not* exhibited explosively, but is communicated through subtle, yet poisonous, words and behavior.

I am talking about such things as sarcasm, nagging, silence, withdrawal, procrastination, sexual affairs, harsh sermons, and "looks that could kill." Many of us have been targets for these types of distorted anger. And when we are honest, we realize we have expressed our negative feelings in these same unhealthy ways.

These backhanded expressions of anger are often unrecognized as being anger. People often use these words and behaviors when they do not realize (or will not admit) they are angry. These are the people of whom it has been said, "They don't get angry but they always get even!" We need to open our eyes and learn to identify these less obvious expressions of anger. First, however, we must describe how anger becomes corrupted.

WHY ANGER GOES BAD

What transforms anger from a potentially creative power into a devastating force? Some people are destructive with their anger because they have no cherished beliefs that prohibit them from openly attacking other persons when they are threatened. They simply don't care whether or not they hurt, ruin, or tear down with their anger. The words "Love your neighbor as yourself" have no ethical meaning for them.

But you are one of the "good folks," one who is called a Christian. You are committed to values that recognize the worth of other persons. It is against your ideals to cause pain and suffering. You do not want to retaliate if you can help it, and guilt seeks you out when you injure others. So how does anger become a problem in your life?

First of all, your past training (which suggests that Christians should not feel angry) may make it difficult for you to admit when anger occurs. It may cause you to pretend you don't get angry. Secondly, your fear of hurting someone if you did get angry can lead you to hide your anger or to swallow it. Psychologists call these two dynamics *denial* and *suppression.*

"Denial" is a word used to describe what happens when a life-event or an emotional response is so threatening that a person refuses to pay attention to it. Anger happens, but the individual is not consciously aware of the negative emotion stirred up inside the self. When you refuse to acknowledge or to be aware of angry feelings, you are denying your anger.

"Suppression" describes what happens when an angry emotional response is recognized, but is so threatening it is immediately pushed out of conscious awareness. Anger is so frightening to many Christians that when it does occur they quickly try to forget it or pretend it was inconsequential, or "hold it in." For our purposes, suppression describes those incidences of anger which you recognize, but because of your discomfort with anger, you try to ignore.

What happens to experiences of anger that you may deny (are unaware of) or suppress (try to ignore)? They stay alive and active in your unconscious! By "unconscious" we are describing the back pockets of your mind where many thoughts, emotions, and other experiences are kept out of sight. A major reason why anger becomes destructive, of course, is that the thoughts and emotions (including anger), which you keep hidden in these "out of sight out of mind" places, continue to affect who you are and what you do.

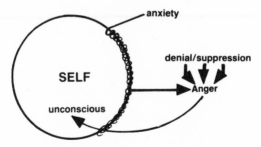

I think the apostle Paul is speaking of this unseen feature of our human nature when he describes his frustration about the way he lived. He called this part of himself, "another law at war with the law of my mind and making me captive to the law of sin" (Rom. 7:23). Paul was aware of the power of this hidden part of life because it kept him from doing things he willed to do and pushed him into thoughts and actions contrary to his values (vs. 15–19).

Please read carefully, for I am not suggesting that the unconscious is evil, nor even the source of evil. I am only pointing out what psychological research has clearly demonstrated: *emotions that are denied or suppressed make up a part of your unconscious mind.* Anger is like energy which doesn't disappear, but can be transformed. Anger, therefore, that is ignored or swallowed is pressed down into this unseen part of the self where it becomes demonic.

Demonic? Yes, I use this word because unrecognized anger is an enemy to our spiritual sensitivity and to our ethical commitments. It can be a stumbling block to the redemptive process and sabotage the abundant life. This anger can be called demonic because it gives birth to hate instead of to nurturing love. It forsakes grace and pushes for punishment. Instead of working toward reconciliation, it breeds alienation. It short-circuits the gift of forgiveness and promotes vengeance.

What gives this unrecognized anger such demonic control in your life? It gets its power because you give up control over anger that you ignore. It is no longer yours to evaluate and take responsibility for. The impact which unrecognized anger has on your entire physical, emotional, social, and spiritual existence is now hidden from you. You have no way of using your rational capacities, your will, or your spiritual resources to guide anger in creative, redemptive, loving directions. Instead, the anger is hidden in your unconscious, acts in isolation, and becomes vulnerable to "the law of sin" which Paul describes.

In short, I am suggesting that every time you and I run from anger, or pretend it does not exist, we have collaborated with sin and made ourselves more vulnerable to the demonic! See if you recognize any of the demonic expressions of anger described below.

ANGER IN DISGUISE

When you imagine someone being angry, you may picture the person throwing dishes, smashing doors, and yelling. If so, you may find it difficult to recognize anger when it is disguised. Yet, much of the anger that people ignore, swallow, or push back into the closets of the mind will sneak out cloaked in another costume.

How do you discover whether a particular behavior of yours is actually camouflaged anger? Pay attention to the *results* of your behavior rather than to its superficial intentions. Illustrated below are some of the most frequent disguises.

HOSTILE HUMOR

A very common disguise for anger is humor. Sarcasm is the most obvious form—its goal is to hurt through ridicule. You probably enjoy "kidding around" at social gatherings. Some teasing remarks are really humorous and witty. Everyone, including the one being kidded, has fun. But at other times the kidding around has a "bite" to it. Someone (maybe you) is "cut" or "put down" by "cute" remarks. Everyone may still laugh, in a socially acceptable way, but you know that the real purpose of these remarks was not to have fun *with* someone, but to poke fun *at* someone through embarrassment, exposure, or hurting the person's feelings. Anger was present in the relationship, whether recognized or not, and revealed itself through attempted humor.

This is a fairly common way in which married couples deal deviously with anger. Have you ever focused people's laughter on your spouse in order to gain some measure of revenge for a recent grievance? Hostile humor is usually used in a social situation where it is difficult for the spouse to respond. If you have used social occasions for veiled expressions of anger, you will understand why you and your spouse felt distant and irritable with each other on the way home. Parents often use hostile humor with their adolescents.

Humor can be an effective expression of affection. When this is its purpose it creates a sense of warmth and closeness. But when humor is used to express anger, it causes alienation.

SEXUALITY

While talking about indirect expressions of hostility in social gatherings, we might as well talk about flirtation. If you and your partner are experiencing conflict in your relationship, you may choose to hurt your spouse through flirtation. Flirtation might be consciously planned. If you are unaware of the hidden anger, however, you might not be aware of its real purpose (to hurt). If your partner accused you of trying to hurt him or her, you would probably deny such intention.

Withholding sex is another deceptive expression of anger which has probably been going on since Adam and Eve. Until recently, depriving the male of sexual satisfaction was one of the few weapons a woman possessed for expressing displeasure. In our day, interestingly, it is just as common for a counselor to work with a marriage in which it is the husband who pouts by refusing sexual encounters with his wife. Refusing to help a person meet a basic need is often an indirect expression of hostility. Sex, of course, happens to be one of the most basic needs. Have you ever expressed your anger toward your spouse by turning off sexually?

If flirtation and/or withholding sex becomes a standard method of expressing anger in a marriage, then either husband or wife might escalate the battle by having an affair. As a marriage and family therapist, I work with many couples whose marriage has been disrupted by an affair. As you know, these affairs are usually *symptomatic* of the problems in the marriage rather than the *cause* of the problems.

What purposes do affairs have? When asked the question, "Why?" spouses who engage in an affair will say things like "for sexual fulfillment," "she understands me," "he listened to me," "he treated me special," or "she was interested in my work." What lies behind these comments? These spouses were feeling some long-standing anger with partners who were not interested in, or concerned about, these specific needs. If the partner's requests go unheard and he or she cannot express anger directly, then an affair is one way of exposing the anger and drawing attention to his or her needs.

Demanding a sexual encounter with your partner can also represent disguised anger. Your conscious intent might be to have a warm, pleasurable encounter, but the deeper motivation is either to gain power by pushing your partner to surrender or to cause conflict by creating resistance. The real goal is to win, not to reconcile.

NAGGING

It is very important to all of us to feel that those people we care for pay attention to our thoughts and ideas. When this does not seem to be the case, we begin to feel unloved and powerless to gain the other person's love. To feel helpless is threatening and anger-producing, particularly if the person you wish to influence represents an important relationship. If a parent, for example, feels powerless to change a child's behavior or does not feel adequate in the relationship, he or she may express anger through constant complaining.

Nagging is fairly safe, but it is also ineffective. Why do

people use this manner of relating? It is a low-risk display of anger. Nagging masquerades as "I'm only trying to help you" or "I'm just reminding you." In truth, it almost always reveals long-standing anger in response to the threat of powerlessness.

SILENCE AND WITHDRAWAL

Silence and withdrawal are two of the most common means by which persons try to conceal anger, yet make sure their displeasure is known. My wife, Judy, and I have shared with many marriage enrichment groups how we used silence and withdrawal to express anger in the early years of our marriage. Both of us were uncomfortable with anger, so we denied and suppressed most of our angry feelings. We could not admit when we were angry, so we did not deal with the anger creatively.

> When Judy was angry she got intensely quiet. She could create silence so thick I could feel it in the air. Her silence threatened me because of my fears about anger and my assumption (at that time) that if she was angry with me, she must not love me. My response to this threat, of course, was to become anxious and angry. Because I considered it unchristian to get angry in return (which to me meant raising my voice or allowing my irritation to show), I withdrew. Sometimes I withdrew into a corner to read, but often I would find socially acceptable reasons to literally leave the apartment. Going to play ball or visiting the library (where I would pretend to study while I tried to figure out what was going on) were two ways to "leave" her. To leave satisfied several needs, although I was unaware of them at the time. First, I could get away from her anger, which was making me uncomfortable. Secondly, I could express my own anger by "punishing" her for being angry with me. I knew that my leaving upset her. When I was really angry and trying "to win" the battle, I would not come home until I knew she would have to be in bed in order to keep her schedule. She really disliked going to bed alone, so my action said in effect, "If

you are going to be angry and not talk to me, then I'll get
back at you by not going to bed with you!''

As you can imagine, we did not experience much love and
intimacy during these times of silence and withdrawal! Anger
had become destructive to our marriage. The sad thing is that
we did not know what was happening. We had not been taught
by the church how to deal with anger and conflict in a relationship. Thankfully we later learned that anger is a natural occurrence in close relationships. Instead of being so afraid of our
anger, we began to take the risk of sharing it with each other
as we did our other thoughts and feelings. We started taking
responsibility for using anger constructively instead of allowing it to rob us of our happiness. We know now that anger has
the potential for increasing intimacy in close relationships. We
will describe this process more extensively in a later chapter.

"I'M SORRY"

Anger is sometimes concealed under mistakes, good intentions, or a poor memory. Since the anger is disguised, the
person expressing anger in one of these ways is probably surprised by his or her action and is regretful. That is why these
incidents are often followed by, "Gee, I'm so sorry."

Have you ever been late, for example, and explained with,
"I'm sorry, but I got held up." Upon further reflection, you
might realize you were "paying someone back" for some word
or action that was threatening to you. Procrastinating may
be passed off with, "Well, I intended to get that done today,
but . . . " You might, however, be saying, "You don't deserve
to have me do something for you today," or "If you hadn't
been nasty to me yesterday, I wouldn't have minded doing that
for you."

The same hostile message may be expressed by forgetting
things. Forgetting, of course, is usually followed by some statement like, "I'm so sorry, I don't know why I forgot to pick up
the milk." The reason might lie in the unresolved conflict that

took place that morning at the breakfast table. Another example I heard in a recent counseling session was, "Did that check have to be deposited today? Oh my, I guess I made a mistake." Yes, she did, and the mistake expressed her longtime anger over how finances are handled by her husband.

MISDIRECTED ANGER

Anger becomes demonic when it is directed toward the wrong target. Angry feelings generated by an interaction with person A or event X are directed instead toward person B or event Y. Of course person B and event Y have been treated unjustly when anger that belongs somewhere else is "dumped" on them. We will examine three common scapegoats of misplaced anger.

ANGER TOWARD THE SELF

The self is often an innocent victim of its own misplaced anger. Your own personhood can become a target for anger that you have not expressed outwardly toward the person or event which poses the real threat. For example, you may feel quite angry but not want anyone to know you are angry. To protect your image you will expend a lot of energy keeping the anger from getting out of the self. What happens? The anger, like a stopped-up sewer, backs up until it spills over inside and poisons the self.

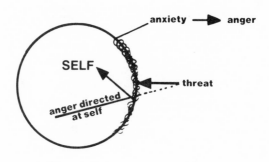

This is most obvious when the anger literally "attacks" your body and becomes physically destructive. Studies of the integral body-mind-emotion connection are revealing. Physical disorders that can be caused or aggravated by internalized anger include cardiovascular problems (such as headaches and high blood pressure), gastrointestinal disorders (such as ulcers and colitis), and many disorders of the skin.

At other times the anger is purposefully aimed toward the self. You may accuse yourself of failures and inadequacies, particularly in response to guilt or shame, as we described earlier. When you hold yourself responsible for events that generate anger (either in other people or yourself), you may end up feeling worthless and undeserving. A major result of this type of self-directed anger is depression. Although sociological and biological factors contribute to depressive moods, it is undeniable that turning your anger in on yourself is a basic cause.

ANGER TOWARD AN INNOCENT PARTY

Another example of misplaced anger is when it is dumped on an innocent object or person. Cartoons abound depicting this little drama. Have you ever become angered at work, but instead of dealing with it there brought it home, where it wreaked havoc on the rest of the family? The family did not deserve it, but they became the victims anyway.

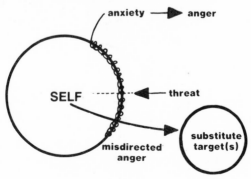

The injustice felt by spouses who serve as substitute targets contributes to many divorces. Untold numbers of children have carried into their adult lives a troublesome, deep-seated rage over the injustice they felt at being substitute targets for parental wrath.

You may direct anger at substitute targets for many reasons. If the person who was the source of threat is very powerful, such as the boss, a policeman, or an authoritarian parent, you may find it too risky to express anger directly toward him or her. Where do you dump it? Often on a scapegoat, such as your wife, husband, child, a golf ball, or a door.

PROJECTING ANGER ONTO OTHERS

An event or experience might be so threatening to you that you cannot consciously or unconsciously claim it as your own. What happens? Occasionally you will "project" these experiences onto others. Projection is a word that describes the process of attributing to others what is really your own. Anger can be misdirected in this manner.

Anger may be so frightening that you cannot accept it as part of your self. Conscious awareness is then distorted, so that the anger is not experienced as something happening inside you, but

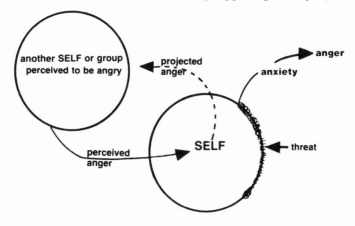

as something originating outside yourself—usually in another person. You may have had the experience of assigning your own anger to some other person, group, or institution and then "finding" it when you think this other person or group is angry with you. Paranoia is the extreme of this dynamic, but suspicion exists to a lesser degree in the day-to-day lives of people who find their unrecognized anger "mirrored" in others.

PORCUPINE SYNDROME

Some people are constantly angry. They seem always on the verge of being mad. You would describe their daily life with words such as harsh, intolerant, demanding, quarrelsome, cruel, bitter, vengeful, and spiteful. They are people with whom you do not want to spend time because their anger is always leaking out. It is often disguised and usually misdirected. I call it the "porcupine syndrome" because if you get near them, you will get pricked.

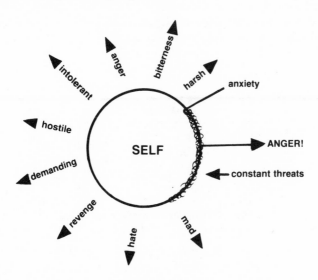

These people relate angrily because they feel constantly threatened on every front. They perceive their selfhood to be under frequent attack. These people are basically insecure and the underlying anxiety keeps them in a constant state of defensiveness. Their alarm system is stuck in the "on" position, keeping them mobilized for attack at any time. In attempting to stay in control, they relate to people by what Karen Horney, in her book *Our Inner Conflicts,* calls "moving against."

EXPLOSIVE ANGER

Anger becomes most obviously destructive when it explodes in brutal rage. Violence has always been a part of American culture (and most of human history). Some people grow up in subcultures where violence is a way of life. When they get irritated or frustrated it is easy to respond with physical outbursts. Other children grow up battered and bruised in homes where physical and/or emotional abuse occurs regularly. Research shows that when they become adults these children are likely to respond to threats in the same manner.

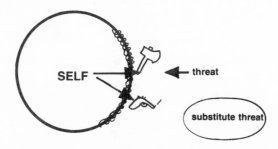

Another group of children are reared without limits and restrictions by parents who are afraid to discipline. These children often learn to use temper tantrums to control their parents. As adults they may continue to use explosive anger to dominate and control others.

Whatever the root cause, violence is usually disastrous because of the damage done both to the victim and to the one who is violent. Reconciliation is rarely achieved by violence. When the Jews came to arrest Jesus in the Garden, Peter's investment in Jesus and his mission was threatened. Peter's angry response was to whip out his sword and attack the slave of the high priest, cutting off the man's ear (John 18:10). Jesus, however, rebuked the disciple's use of violence (although, interestingly enough, he did not chastise him for feeling threatened and angry). "But Jesus said, 'No more of this!' And he touched his ear and healed him" (Luke 22:51). Matthew quotes Jesus in this same incident saying, "All who take the sword will perish by the sword" (Matt. 26:52).

One of the most cruel expressions of hostility is rape. Few people still think that rape is primarily motivated by sexual needs. Stored-up anger, often at women, is ruthlessly discharged (usually at a substitute target) with the intent of hurting. It is also important to most rapists to overpower and dominate their victim in a show of strength and exaggerated masculinity.

STOREHOUSE ANGER

Each of you can remember situations that elicited more anger than you would have expected. Can you recall such a situation? An incident deserving about 10 kilowatts of anger, but you felt (and maybe expressed) 100 kilowatts' worth of hostility? What happened? Where did the extra 90 kilowatts of "heat" come from? Probably from the storehouse where unexpressed, unreconciled anger has been festering. Theodore Isaac Rubin, in his *The Angry Book,* calls this the "slush-fund."

What actually happens to the anger from the past? All the answers are not known, but we know that anger felt in the past can be felt again in the present. It is not so much like a boiling pot full of anger residing in a deep recess of the body, although when it gets activated we can often feel it physically. It is more like a memory bank where we file hostilities, irritations, threats, and injustices from the past. When a current situation is shaped something like the past event, it prompts a "recall process" in which the previous anger is remembered. If that anger was not expressed effectively or was not creatively resolved, then the memory may evoke the same physical or emotional response that occurred at the time of the original event. Anger experienced and expressed at any given moment may hook a memory (from this psychic warehouse where such memories are stored), making the present anger much stronger (hotter) than the present situation warrants.

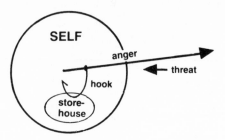

You may find that storehouse anger is interrupting, even destroying, a present relationship.

> Linda is aware that the anger she expresses at her husband is usually undeserved. She gets furious with him for not "paying attention" when she is talking, not "noticing what I do," and "taking me for granted." Yet, when she reflects on their relationship she describes him as a sensitive, thoughtful person who spends time with her, listens patiently, and compliments her work. "I know he loves me," she says tearfully. "Why do I get so angry?"

Further counseling revealed that Linda spent most of her childhood and teenage years trying to get the attention and approval of her father. He was a competent, respected physician. Linda admired him and was proud to be his daughter, but his schedule allowed little time for her. He also was a perfectionist and was often critical of Linda. Despite her efforts to get his attention and earn his approval, she was never able to feel that she was important to him. This constantly frustrated and hurt her. By her teenage years her anger toward him was strong, even though she rarely expressed it.

Somewhere in the back of her mind, Linda still remembers the attention and approval she desperately wanted while growing up. When her husband gives the slightest hint of not paying full attention or giving complete approval, it reminds her inner self of this previous hurt. Anger orginally felt toward her dad, which has filled up her storehouse, is "hooked" and she gets very angry. Linda is working at recognizing and expressing this old anger more responsibly and making progress toward separating yesterday's anger from today's.

CONCLUSION

It probably does not surprise you to think of anger being destructive. The above pages, however, may have expanded your awareness of the many unrecognized ways in which anger is destructive. Now we move to a discussion of the positive contributions that anger can make to our Christian pilgrimage.

Chapter 5
Anger Can Be Helpful

What do you think about this chapter title? Are you offended by the suggestion that anger could have any positive role in your life? Anger gets so much "bad press" and is, in fact, such a potentially dangerous part of human nature that it may be difficult for you to imagine anger as a friend. If you have always perceived anger to be an enemy, or been exposed to anger only in its destructive forms, then the idea of anger as a guide on your spiritual pilgrimage will seem ridiculous. If you have read this far, however, you are probably curious enough to explore the possibility, so follow me a little further.

ANGER A DANGER SIGNAL

As we have seen, anger (along with fear) is an emotion that springs from the anxiety we experience when our personhood is threatened. Anger fills an important role in our life as an indicator of danger. Anger motivates our defensive and aggressive responses to these threats. It is part of our survival system provided by the Creator. Some say that although this defense system was necessary in the days when humans actually had to fight wild animals or escape from them and from hostile neighbors, it is not very helpful now when you and I do not physically have to defend ourselves. It is pointed out that in modern life the chemical changes which occur in our bodies create ulcers, high blood pressure, and colitis because we don't "use up" these chemicals by physically fighting or escaping.

To some degree this is true, but we need to note that human beings are not completely free from threats to their physical lives. People who are escaping from a fire, struggling to save someone from drowning, running from a rapist, or fighting for their lives in an intensive care unit need the extra physical and emotional boost provided by fear and anger. When a person is threatened by a serious disease, the body's preparation for defense may be a key ingredient in survival. The anger can be appropriately focused on the disease and motivate the person to resist. Anger is an important part of the will to live.

Furthermore, we would be oversimplifying the life of ancient human beings if we think the only threats that they had to confront were physical. Certainly those ancient humans were also in conflict over ideas, relationships, and self-integrity. It is also true that throughout history human beings have had to struggle with spiritual anxieties, which we will describe in the next chapter.

In the twentieth century, of course, we are most often threatened in nonphysical ways. While learning to deal with the bodily changes (which may seem unnecessary), you must remember that the anxiety you feel in response to a threat (including fear and anger) is still a good gift from God. Why? Anger is the early warning system which indicates that something is threatening your progress toward an abundant life. God not only wants you to survive physically, but is interested also in your emotional, mental, and spiritual well-being. Many things happen in life which can keep you from growing and developing into what God would have you be. You need to be aware of those forces which would keep you immature, dependent, or alienated. Anger is a signal that these forces are threatening your search to be a mature spiritual person. This chapter illustrates some of the ways in which anger serves as a positive force in our search for the abundant life.

ANGER: A PUSH TOWARD INDEPENDENCE

The dependence-independence struggle is one place where anger can be a friend. Anger, you see, can be a warning that a person is dependent in an unhealthy way. It is a rule of thumb in human relationships that anger is usually present when a person is unnecessarily dependent. Anger may motivate a person to move out of a dependent position which is keeping him or her from reaching maturity.

Achieving independence is an important part of becoming a whole person. The person who does not accomplish this separation from his or her parents by the end of adolescence will have a difficult time becoming a mature adult. Becoming independent means reaching a degree of autonomy that is characterized by the ability to make one's own decisions, taking responsibility for oneself, adopting a personal value system, and establishing a personal identity separate from that of one's parents.

This is sometimes called the process of "individuation." It begins early in life as children learn to stand "over against" their parents. From the two-year-old's "No!" through the teenager's "I'm old enough to make up my own mind!" children grow toward this independence. Guiding this process, so it doesn't happen either too slowly or too quickly, is one of the tasks of parenting. Some parents, however, block their child's movement toward independence. They may be frightened by this process of separation. Or they may have a strong need to control their children. Children usually respond in two ways to this overpossessiveness. Some children express their anger in response to this threat by open rebellion. They fight for independence by turning their anger outward against the parents who seem to be blocking their children's path toward selfhood. Other children are more dominated by fear, so they deny and suppress their anger. They try to be perfectly obedient to their overprotective parents and usually stay unnaturally dependent and immature.

Daniel was twenty-seven years old, single, and in his third year of a graduate program. His major professor sent him to me because he was in danger of flunking out of the program despite his outstanding ability. Daniel came willingly because he was concerned that he was "so depressed all the time" that he couldn't concentrate. He was worried about what he would do after graduation. He was about to graduate with a master's degree but did not like the jobs available in his field. When I asked why he didn't pursue a job he liked, he said, "Mother would have a fit!"

It turned out that Daniel was preparing for a vocation he didn't like because it was the career his mother had been planning for him since he was a child. As a dutiful son, he had been faking interest in this profession, hoping he could learn to like it and satisfy his mother. Over a period of time Daniel told me his story.

He was an only child born late in the life of his parents, who had been told earlier they would probably not have children. His mother told him often of his difficult birth and her feeling that Daniel was a "special gift from God." She overprotected him from the beginning and continued to treat him as a frail child. She mothered by "smothering" him! Daniel revealed that "Mom and Dad don't get along too well," which may explain why, as he said, "I'm her whole life!" She monitored his every move, listened to his phone calls, grilled him about his activities, gave constant advice, made most of his decisions, and became very upset when he did not follow her wishes. Daniel grew up believing that his mother's happiness was his responsibility (a heavy burden for a child). He was always "good" (meaning dependent) so that she would not be upset.

At first Daniel was unaware of the anger he felt toward his mother. However, as he continued to recount story after story of his mother's domination he spoke with more and more anger. Although he found it very difficult to share any of this anger with his mother, he could share it with me. Slowly he began to realize how his desire to be a mature adult was being seriously delayed by his dependency. Finally, after he had months of counseling, the anger motivated him to begin breaking out of this dependent relationship. He began to consider his own vocational goals, date women whether his mother liked them or not, keep some parts of his life secret from her, and refused to go home every other weekend.

In this situation anger was an appropriate response to a threat to self-esteem. Daniel thought very little of himself because he was such "a mommy's boy." The anger signaled the truth that his development as an adult was being threatened by his mother's control. The anger, when finally recognized and accepted, became Daniel's friend because it motivated his defense (and later an offense) against this threat.

ANGER AS AN "IDOL DETECTOR"

It may come as a surprise to you, but anger is an excellent "idol detector." What in the world is *that?* you wonder. Well, an idol detector is something that helps you realize when something from this world has been moved into the center of your life, the position you have supposedly reserved for the living God.

You and I are committed to the first commandment, "You shall have no other Gods before me" (Ex. 20:3). Yet we constantly take the common stuff of life and worship it as if it were a god. That's bad enough, but it is complicated by the fact that we often fail to recognize when we have created an idol. We need help in detecting them. I suggest that just as a metal detector points to buried treasure, anger can help uncover idols. Let me describe how you can use anger to help track down your idols.

First, you must remember that idols constantly need defending. Why? Because in reality they are false gods which are not capable of being as significant and meaningful as you and I want them to be. They cannot bring real joy, nor provide peace of mind, nor carry our hopes and dreams, nor even meet our basic human needs. Therefore, idols are always being exposed by events which point out their deficiencies. When we are depending on an idol, we don't like to admit its weaknesses. Therefore, when idols are exposed, we get threatened → anxious → angry. Since idols cannot defend themselves, we end up defending them with our anger.

How does anger serve as an idol detector? When you pay careful attention to the evaluation of your threat → anxiety → anger response, you will often be painfully aware of the fact that you are threatened because of your overinvestment in some thing or person. A human attachment has become so strong that it has become an idolatrous relationship.

ANGER UNCOVERS GUILT AND SHAME

In Chapter 2 we described the type of anxiety created when you violate your value system (guilt) or fall short of your ideal self (shame). You know what a terrible experience it is to realize that you have broken a pledge, hurt someone, cheated, told a lie, acted illegally, or disobeyed your conscience. The sense of guilt and failure can be overwhelming. It is so uncomfortable, in fact, that we often deny or suppress the feeling of guilt. It is easy to rationalize guilt by explaining it away, or denying responsibility for what happened.

At this point anger can be a spiritual guide. If guilt is present (whether recognized or not), it is obvious that a threat has occurred. When you are threatened, you know that anger will be present in your anxiety. Therefore, if you are sensitive to your anger and evaluate it carefully, you might recognize guilt that otherwise would be ignored. If the anxiety you experience is indeed guilt, you can take steps to face this threat to your value system. In other words, guilt may exist, but the only sign of its existence is the anger. If you pay attention to the anger, you can face up to the guilt and take responsibility for the incident that caused the threat in the first place.

Marilyn and Ken brought their seventeen-year-old daughter to see me at the counseling center. The daughter had recently told them she was having sexual intercourse with her boyfriend. Marilyn and Ken were very angry, which is not unusual for parents in this situation. Marilyn, however, continued to be so furious that I could not see the three together. So I saw the parents separately and continued to ask why so much hostility. Finally, Marilyn broke down in tears as she confessed that this seventeen-year-old daughter had been conceived out of wedlock.

Marilyn had been so frightened and embarrassed by her sexual act that she had pushed it far into the back of her mind. She had both violated her own moral code and fallen short of her ideal self. She tried to cope with this threatening experience by suppressing her memory of it. Forgetting it kept her from dealing with the guilt. The anger that was part of her anxiety, however, had been "hooked" by the daughter's confession. Suddenly the anger that Marilyn had originally felt toward herself, had erupted at the daughter. Her daughter's behavior was threatening, but the bigger threat was Marilyn's own guilt. She finally faced her guilt and came to accept God's forgiveness. Anger had served as a spiritual guide.

Knowing the connection between anger and guilt allows you to include this possibility when evaluating a time of anger. When trying to understand a particular incident of anger, you can ask: "Could I be feeling guilty? Is the threat that is making me so anxious related to something I have done for which I feel ashamed, embarrassed, or compromised?" The answer may reveal that the anxiety *is* related to guilt. This discovery can lead you to a renewed spiritual vitality through repentance, confession, acceptance of forgiveness, and restitution.

If Marilyn's anger had not been recognized and evaluated, her denial of guilt would have continued unnoticed and she would have missed the opportunity for reconciliation with both God and neighbor (her daughter). The guilt would have remained and would have continued to be problematic. Anger, therefore, served a spiritual purpose when it enabled her to claim her guilt and take responsible action.

LOVE AND INJUSTICE

Wrath! Not a pretty word—one I find myself responding to with a shudder. But there it is, sticking out all through Scripture, usually describing God's reaction to some human situation. During the period in my life when I believed anger was the opposite of love, it was difficult to imagine the God of love being "filled with wrath." So I didn't pay much attention to the word. When I learned that anger and love often go together, however, I realized an interesting thing about God's love: *it gets angry at injustice!* God loves you and me enough to get angry with us when we treat each other unjustly.

The Bible speaks often of God's anger toward those who hurt their fellow humans. Jesus, for example, when talking about children's faith and humbleness, added the comment,

> "Whoever receives one such child in my name receives me; but whoever causes one of these little ones who believe in me to sin, it would be better for him to have a great millstone fastened around his neck and to be drowned in the depth of the sea." (Matt. 18:5-6)

In other words, treat my children kindly, with goodness and mercy, or else! Can you sense the anger Jesus would feel toward anyone who did not treat children kindly?

On God's behalf the prophets called for justice. You have heard since childhood those words from the Lord spoken through Amos, "But let justice roll down like waters, and righteousness like an ever-flowing stream" (Amos 5:24). Furthermore, we are told that God gets angry with those who do *not* practice justice. Amos, for example, constantly expressed God's displeasure at robbery and violence (3:10), oppression of the poor (5:11), apathy toward the needy (5:12), and cheating (8:5). Not only are we reminded of God's anger at injustice, but Amos goes farther by telling us to feel the same way. He calls for those who worship God to "Hate evil, and love good, and establish justice" (5:15).

We have seen that anger is created when something threatens the people and ideas that are important to us. We do not want to indicate that all these threats are bad. In fact, many things *should* threaten Christians. You and I should be committed to a value system that includes justice for all people. We should be committed to fairness, honesty, and respect and stand opposed to prejudice, bigotry, cheating, and manipulation. When situations occur in which injustice is obvious, Christians *should* feel threatened and experience anger. At our best, you and I should be sensitive to human freedom and feel threatened when that freedom is compromised.

To be angry at injustice (oppression, cheating, prejudice, and other evils) is an appropriate expression of love. Anger inspired by love should motivate us to cry out for righteousness. Anger that grows out of love leads us to fight for freedom, to challenge the oppressors, to do battle for others who are being denied the abundant life.

If you do not pay attention to your anger, you may miss the injustices that are appropriately threatening your Christian values. This means you will not be able to respond to the injustice. You will have no energy to motivate you, no indignation to give you courage to take the risks of challenging evil.

I am convinced that a major reason for the church's reluctance to be a champion of justice is our fear of getting angry. Why aren't more Christians active in basic issues of justice like racism, sexism, and civil rights? I think one reason is that they are so fearful of feeling angry that they desensitize themselves to the ethical issues which *should* threaten them. If we allowed ourselves to be threatened by injustice, the anger could empower us to take ethical action. What about you? If you are not actively "hating evil, loving good, and establishing justice," ask yourself, "Why not?" Perhaps you are not tuned in to love's call for justice. But, more likely, you will discover that you don't *act* because you don't *feel!* If you allowed yourself to *feel* the anger, maybe your experience with God, and your commitment to love, would allow you to have more compassion on others and strive against those forces which abuse, oppress, hurt, and destroy your brothers and sisters in this world.

Chapter 6
Why Christians
Need to Face Anger

An understanding of anger that captures the basic thread of agreement which runs through the various biological, psychological, and sociological theories, was presented in Chapter 2. Now we must raise the question, "Does this explanation of anger fit the Christian faith's understanding of human experience?" How do Christian beliefs about what it means to be human fit with what the social scientists have found in their research?

I believe that the Christian faith supports the understanding of anger presented earlier, but it also adds breadth and depth to this concept. When we take the spiritual aspects of human existence seriously, we expand our interpretation and understanding of anger. In fact, we will see that anger is more closely related to our spiritual lives than is commonly recognized. The opportunity for increased spiritual awareness is a major reason why Christians need to face their anger.

BEING HUMAN

Our Christian understanding of human life confirms this concept of anger because we recognize human finitude. Unlike some religious groups, Christians have always maintained the belief that human beings are "finite." Most Christian thinkers have insisted on a high view of humankind, recognizing us as the crown of creation and celebrating that we carry within us the image of God. Yet we are "finite"!

What does this word mean? It comes from the past participle of the Latin verb *finire* and means "to be limited." Dictionary definitions include words such as "transient," "impermanent," and "limited" along with phrases such as "having boundaries" and "existing for a limited time only." Christians who use this word "finite" do so to describe the difference between humans (who are limited) and God (who is limitless). We are the creatures (having boundaries) and God is Creator (without boundaries).

You and I are limited, for example, in our knowledge. We cannot see the future clearly, nor do we know the past completely. Even if we used all of our considerable brain power, we can know only a tiny fraction of what there is to know in the universe.

Related to this limitation are the boundaries of space set by the "physicalness" of our existence. Our selfhood is dependent on our bodies. Certainly we believe that humans are self-transcendent in amazing ways. We can see with our mind's eye and travel in our imaginations, but our bodies (therefore our selves) are limited to being completely in only one place at a time. Furthermore, our bodies are vulnerable to accident and disease, pain and suffering, which brings us to the final boundary—time!

Yes, we are limited in time. Humans are "transient" and "impermanent," having only a relatively short span of years in which to live. Despite our fantasies we are not immortal. The most obvious evidence of our finitude is that we get old and die.

What has this to do with anger? Each of us gets threatened because of our limits and boundaries. Being able to imagine life without boundaries heightens our awareness of them and produces other types of threats. The unknown, for example, is one source of threat. The fact that our bodies, upon which we depend for our very existence, are fragile and vulnerable is the source of other threats.

> I found Bart, a middle-aged dentist, in the Coronary Care Unit. He wanted to talk about his anxiety. He had experienced some heart trouble a few weeks earlier and was hospitalized for tests which revealed no cause for alarm. Today, however, while taking a walk after lunch, he suffered a heart attack. After he gave himself oxygen at his own office, his wife drove him to the emergency room at the local hospital. Until the medical personnel took over, Bart stayed relatively calm and rational. However, after he was left lying alone in the examining room, he became extremely anxious. As he told me, "I knew that each breath could be my last. For the first time in my life I knew that I could die!" Death was no longer something that happened to other people or after you were old—it was a present threat. Bart's response to this realization, of course, was to become anxious and fearful. Bart wanted to know, "Is something wrong with my faith? Why am I so scared?"

From Bart's point of view his Christian faith should have protected him from this sense of fear and impending doom. His faith had never encountered such a frightening event, but he had "always expected to be strong" in the face of such a trauma. Bart was scared because his life was in danger. Death is an unknown. He was concerned about what would happen to him "out there" and what would happen to his wife and children "here" without him. Life seemed out of control, and Bart, like others in such a situation, was threatened. Did he get angry? Yes! He was angry at the tests, which he thought might have caused the attack. Furthermore, he was angry with the doctor who had insisted he have those particular tests. Bart also felt angry with himself for smoking and for living under too much stress.

Like Bart, you cannot live without being threatened by your finitude. You experience anxiety in response to these threats, which means, of course, that *you cannot live without experiencing anger.* Can such a statement be defended theologically? Obviously I would say yes. It is from within a Christian understanding of the nature and meaning of human existence that I point out that threat → anxiety → anger are part of what it means to be human.

SPIRITUAL ANXIETY

We now ask the question, "What can Christian knowledge about human experience contribute to our understanding of anger?" From a Christian point of view, the understanding of anger presented in Chapter 2 is still incomplete because it does not take into consideration the spiritual dimensions of human nature. By spiritual dimensions, I refer to our recognition of the existence of Holy Other, our awareness of the reality of death, our expectation that life has meaning, our awareness of our unique potential, and our feeling of responsibility for this uniqueness.

These spiritual dimensions of human existence pose *spiritual* threats which lie behind those already described. We must therefore add a significant development to our understanding, a revision which recognizes that behind the more obvious physical, social, and psychological threats to our selfhood lie deeper threats that are theological and spiritual in nature.

Christian thinkers have constantly reminded us of the fact that anxiety is basic to being human. Paul Tillich, for example, in his book *The Courage to Be,* points out that to exist as human beings is necessarily to experience anxiety. Why? Because, says Tillich, it creates a deep sense of anxiety when we experience our own finitude. Like other Christian thinkers, he believes that *all humans* experience this type of anxiety, it is part of the human experience. This means, of course, that all humans experience anger! Therefore, to deny that you experience anger would be to deny that you are finite and, in effect, claim to be like God!

DEATH

Perhaps the most basic of these spiritual anxieties is the fear of death. We have mentioned the threat you feel to your physical self from accident, disease, nuclear weapons, pollution, and tornadoes. But why do you feel threatened by these seemingly fateful occurrences? Because they have the potential to kill you. If you think about it, these phenomena would not have the same power to create anxiety if death did not lurk in the background.

"Hey, wait a minute," you might say, "doesn't our faith protect us from this anxiety because of our belief in immortality and resurrection?" No, your faith does not do away with this anxiety. It may, of course, provide hope and courage. Faith can help you deal with anxiety in the presence of death when your hope is placed in the power of God's promise to overcome death. Faith does not protect you from the anxiety that humans undergo in the presence of death, but it does provide the courage that enables you to overcome the anxiety.

Yes, even Christians are anxious in the face of death, the death of those they love as well as their own death. In his book *Learn to Grow Old,* Paul Tournier recalls a conversation with his aging sister after she had suffered cardiac failure.

> She had really believed, she said, that she was going to die. She had experienced terrible anxiety. And now she was questioning me because she felt ashamed of her anxiety, which she looked upon as a lack of faith. Should a Christian believer like her not have faced death with serenity? (P. 222)

Tournier, as both a Christian and a medical doctor with training in psychiatry, also believes that anxiety concerning death is a universal experience. Every person experiences this anxiety whether consciously or not. Tournier's acceptance of this anxiety as a part of creaturehood shows in his answer to his sister.

> Christian faith, I said to her, does not involve repressing
> one's anxiety in order to appear strong. On the contrary,
> it means recognizing one's weakness, accepting the in-
> ward truth about oneself, confessing one's anxiety . . . and
> still to believe. . . . I believe that there is more peace to
> be found in acceptance of human anxiety than in the hope
> for a life or an old age freed from anxiety. (P. 222)

Why call death a spiritual threat? Because death carries the
possibility of ending your existence, not only in this life but
forever. "But we believe we have received the gift of eternal
life," you say. Right, but this is a belief you hold by faith
because of your spiritual experience. You are also a rational
creature, however, and from a scientific point of view you
cannot prove life after death. Recently you have read of people
who have experienced death in a hospital setting and were
"brought back to life." They described a beautiful and assuring
picture of what lies beyond, but we do not know with any
certainty what kind of experience this describes.

Death remains a mystery, an unknown feature of human
existence. Death is a spiritual threat because it challenges your
beliefs, your religious ideas, as something that cannot be
proved. Death is welcomed by some aging persons, by some
who are in great pain, and by others who are emotionally tired
of life. For you and me, however, death (at our age and stage
of life) is a threat. As depth psychology has pointed out, most
humans perceive their selfhood as immortal. You obviously
want to enjoy life, but you have no guarantee (except by faith)
past this life.

MEANINGLESSNESS AND THE PROBLEM OF EVIL

A second spiritual anxiety described by Tillich is the anxiety
you and I experience in the face of meaninglessness. I have
described the threat created by such things as cancer, automo-
bile wrecks, hurricanes, and chemicals, because they can cause
death. However, they also threaten us because they seem to be
evil things which have no meaning. Frank and Virginia's six-

teen-year-old son killed himself with a rifle. Paula was a random victim of an unknown male rapist in back of the grocery store where she works. Gregory has been blind since birth because his mother had German measles early in her pregnancy. These events do not make sense. They are absurd, meaningless accidents to these people.

Who among us does not experience anger in the face of the senseless? As a Christian, sensitized by God's love, you may feel more anger than anyone. Why? You are committed to love and wholeness. You do not like to see pain and suffering. When evil appears, you feel that an injustice has occurred, and since you are a Christian, *injustice should threaten you and make you angry.*

We also get threatened when crude, ugly, destructive events happen in a world watched over by a loving God. Traditional Christian faith maintains that God is in control and that "in everything God works for good with those who love him" (Rom. 8:28). But many things happen in life that make us question the truthfulness of such a belief. These events become spiritual threats. Down deep, whether you are consciously aware of it or not, you may wonder if your faith is accurate. Doubt gnaws at you, even if only for a brief moment. "Is any One in charge here?" "Is there a grand plan?" "Does God really know or care about what is happening here?" This threat to your spiritual self (because your beliefs about the nature of God are threatened) creates anxiety which leads to anger.

John Claypool, then a pastor in Louisville, Kentucky, shared such an experience in a sermon titled "The Basis of Hope." This sermon was preached after doctors found that his eight-year-old daughter had leukemia.

> The first thing I have to share may surprise you a bit, but I must in all honesty confess it, and it is that I have found no answer to the deepest question of this experience. When I first heard this diagnosis and went out alone to cry, I raised the question anyone would ask, namely,

"Why has this happened? Why do little girls get leukemia? Why is there leukemia at all? Why is there sickness
and suffering and pain and death in a world that is supposed to be the creation of an all-good and an all-power-
ful God?" These are age-old questions, and I searched the
pages of the Bible and my books of theology and my
memory and my Christian experience, and I found no
neat and tidy answer to lay such a question to rest. I am
already familiar with most of the attempted solutions to
this mystery of evil and pain, and every one of them left
something to be desired and left the question right where
it had started, namely, a dark mystery for which there is
no satisfactory explanation. Therefore, let me say at the
very beginning that if you expect me to share an answer
to this problem of pain, or give you some explanation of
how this sort of thing happens and why, you are in for a
disappointment. Up to this moment, in the Bible, in theology, in my experience—nowhere have I found an answer that settles all the questions or accounts for all the
nuances of this tragic occurrence.

Such anxiety automatically sparks the anger that gets us ready
to fight this intruder called death. We would strangle death
with our bare hands if we could get hold of it. But death is
not a tangible enemy which we can lay hold of. We also fear
death and would escape it if we could. And in our society
there are numerous ways in which individuals try to escape,
such as worshiping youth and vitality, hiding the aging process, using drugs and alcohol to anesthetize the self, and iso-
lating those who are dying in nursing homes and hospitals.

Just as death cannot be ignored, you cannot escape the
spiritual threat of meaninglessness. Faith cannot protect you
from anxiety about the apparent meaninglessness of much that
happens. Faith does, however, provide answers that are helpful
and, most important, faith can supply the courage necessary to
stand and face meaninglessness. Your trust in the living God
who loves you can lead you to hope in the ultimate meaningful-
ness of life, whether or not there is an answer or an explanation
for every event.

GUILT AND CONDEMNATION

A third spiritual threat grows out of our existence as responsible creatures. I described earlier how threats to self-esteem are a major source of anxiety and anger. A Christian's understanding of human existence, however, adds a deeper dimension to this understanding.

Numerous theologians have pointed out that each human being is created with unique potential. Furthermore, each individual is aware, at some level of consciousness, of his or her responsibility for fulfilling this uniqueness. When you and I make decisions which act to destroy or violate this potential, our internal response is the spiritual anxiety of guilt and shame and the feelings of self-rejection and self-hate.

Behind this guilt and shame is the threat of God's condemnation. What do we mean by condemnation? We are describing the spiritual fear that the Creator would find us to be unworthy and would reject our personhood. If you have ever questioned whether or not you are acceptable to God, you know that it creates quite a threat to the spiritual self, followed by anxiety and anger.

The experience of a friend of mine is helpful in understanding the impact of the fear of condemnation. Furthermore, his experience serves as a good illustration of all three spiritual anxieties.

> Jack came to me because of strong anger which he was expressing verbally and physically to his wife. He also recognized that anger might be behind his chronic depressiveness and self-defeating procrastination. After we explored his present situation, we used his anger as a "diagnostic window" and found a storehouse of anger related to the death of his mother when he was only sixteen. She had been sick for six years with illnesses that caused severe pain, irrational behavior, and loss of consciousness. Occasionally Jack found her on the floor after school or heard her in pain at night. He often felt angry toward her for being sick all the time and sometimes

wished she would die. These hostile feelings made him feel extremely guilty. Tragically for Jack, his mother died on a day he had gotten so anxious and angry about her illness that he left unannounced and went to the beach. He felt ashamed that he had not been "man enough" to stay by her side. His guilt increased because he assumed he could have saved her life by being home.

Obviously Jack faced spiritual threats. At sixteen he had to face the tough, fearful questions about death we described earlier. His search for answers led to a "conversion" experience three months after his mother's death. But the threat of death remains. At deepest levels he still fears that death is the end of existence. Although he knows about resurrection and eternal life, he has not incorporated them into his experience of faith. Since he has no satisfactory response to this spiritual threat, he faces constant anxiety and anger.

The question of meaninglessness was also a threatening issue. Jack said, in a letter I asked him to write to his mother: "I am angry that you didn't get the full threescore and ten . . . that you deserved. . . . I don't recall that you ever did anyone any harm. . . . You deserved better." Why God let his mother suffer and allowed a sixteen-year-old boy to lose his parent were questions Jack has asked for a long time. He still wonders whether there is a righteous God in control.

Most significantly, Jack believed that God held him responsible for his mother's death. He also wrote in the letter: "I am angry at how we all seemed to just watch it happen. . . . I'm sorry I wasn't at the house when you died. . . . The only coping device I knew was to run away. I'm sorry for that, I hope you understand." Jack is continually threatened → anxious → angry by his fear that God's condemnation was final.

It was important to Jack to uncover these spiritual anxieties. If he had not been willing to do some detective work with his anger, he could not have discussed these spiritual concerns. Now he has been able to bring his religious knowledge and experience to bear on these questions. As this storehouse anger is identified and shared, Jack is better able to recognize his spiritual anxieties.

As he becomes more aware of his fear of death, he is able to develop a "faithing" stance which provides him with more courage in the face of death. Recognizing his anger at a seemingly meaningless event gave him the freedom to express the anger he feels toward God but was unable to express at sixteen. He has shared his hurt, pain, and sense of injustice with God.

Finally, he has confessed the guilt and shame he has felt since he was sixteen. The experience of forgiveness and acceptance has helped immeasurably in reducing his anxiety and the resulting anger. His wife is no longer a target for misplaced anger from the storehouse. Like the rest of us, Jack will continue to be anxious and angry because of his finitude, but his faith is now mobilized to provide the hope and courage to face anger more creatively.

SUMMARY

Now we have discussed the most significant spiritual anxieties and the anger which goes with any anxiety. We know that since anxiety is an unescapable part of being human, anger also has to be present. Christians who are willing to face anger have the possibility of expanding their spiritual awareness. Why? Because honestly facing our anxiety over death, guilt, and meaninglessness gives us a chance to wrestle with our faith and therefore with God.

"With God?" you ask. Yes, because sooner or later, just like Jack, the anger you experience in the face of these spiritual threats will be anger you feel toward God! A good portion of the anger I hear from people, even when it is misplaced onto others, is anger which they feel consciously or unconsciously at God. Therefore, an important reason for you to deal openly with your anger is to protect your relationship with God.

ANGER TOWARD GOD

The biblical Hebrews, as we have seen earlier, accepted the fact that people get angry. They also recognized that human beings get angry with God. This seemed such a natural part of life that they provided a place in their worship for expressing their anger. As you read those psalms called "the Laments" (Ps. 13; 44; and 74, e.g.) you will hear their anger. The Israelites felt free to express their strong emotions to God whether they were grateful, fearful, grieved, or angry. Jesus quoted one of these psalms (Ps. 22:1) on the cross when he cried out, "My God, my God, why hast thou forsaken me?" (Mark 15:34).

These psalms are part of our Christian heritage, but rarely do we use them in our worship. Why? Early in Christian history the church began to teach that believers should not get angry with God. This teaching reflected the growing belief that anger (and all other emotions as well) were part of humanity's "carnal nature" and opposed to spirituality. As people began to look more and more on anger as a sign of evil, they became less willing to admit their anger toward God or to express anger in worship. To be angry with God became a sign of spiritual immaturity. It was assumed that anger with God was a sign of prideful rebellion, signaling that the individual was not accepting God's will. Some even suggested that God had little tolerance for human anger and might strike back.

As we described in Chapter 1, this view of anger is still believed by many Christians and in many churches. I learned in childhood (as you probably did) that being angry with God was not acceptable. I was supposed to love God, praise God, thank God, and even make requests of God, but getting angry with God seemed like something only "bad" kids would do. As a young adult I began to question this teaching from an intellectual point of view. My understanding of God grew and

I stopped relating to God as "a super-parent" in the sky who would not tolerate back talk or insubordination. My religious experience no longer allowed me to imagine that God would be threatened or overwhelmed by my emotions, not even anger. This part of my faith, however, was not tested (outside my mind) until my son was born.

> On a Sunday afternoon, as Judy began her seventh month of pregnancy, she began passing clear liquid. A hurried call to her obstetrician revealed that the water sac membranes had ruptured and labor would begin soon. We were to go right to the hospital. We were quite frightened by this turn of events. In my ignorance I could only assume that if labor was beginning at the end of six months, something was wrong—our first child was either dead or dying.
>
> As we rushed to the hospital I tried to remain calm in order to keep Judy from getting too worried. But I was threatened by the probable (in my mind) loss of our child, and also by potential complications for Judy. Fear for Judy was dominant until she was safely in the labor room under the doctor's care. Then I became aware of my anger. During one of the examinations I left the labor room and went to the chapel. Within my prayer, I took the risk of expressing my anger to God. I voiced my sense of injustice that this little one should be endangered and shared my anger that our hopes and dreams seemed to be crashing around us.

I had raised "Why?" questions with God before, but had never expressed the anger until this moment. Thankfully, Scott was developed enough to survive his premature birth. The first few days were very critical, but after a six-week stay he came home from the hospital and we resumed a normal life. I was grateful not only for his life but also for the "testing" of my relationship with God. I had no doubt that God accepted and understood the anger in my prayers as well as the fear, concern, petition, and (later) gratitude. My "faithing" experience was affirmed. My spiritual awareness expanded and my commitment deepened.

If personal relationships are to reach their potential for love and intimacy, they must be characterized by open, honest communication. You know that you only reveal your deepest thoughts and feelings to those you care for a great deal, such as your spouse and close friends. You don't share your whole self with those you do not trust or do not know well. You also know that a relationship between two normal people, such as marriage partners or parents and children, is bound to spark some conflict. It is clear that when this anger is dealt with openly and straightforwardly it promotes (and even creates) intimacy. This is not only true in our human relationships but in our relationship with God. The opposite is also true. When anger generated in a close relationship is not shared, alienation and mistrust result.

One relationship often alienated by anger is the one between an individual and God. It is amazing how often I talk with people who feel angry toward God but are inhibited in sharing this anger because they have been taught that to express anger to God is disrespectful. Do we think God is threatened by our anger?

If you have been influenced by the idea that anger is unacceptable to God, then you probably have trouble dealing with this part of human experience in your devotional life. In the early centuries of church history, men and women training for religious vocations were taught not to pray when they were angry. This idea continues into the present and particularly affects us if we are handling anger poorly. My family, for example, usually expresses a prayer of thanksgiving and commitment at the dinner table. If we have been fussing with each other, it feels awkward to have our prayer. If the family member whose turn it is to pray is angry, he or she might feel "not in the mood to pray" and ask another to take the turn.

You may have experienced a lack of freedom and spontaneity in your prayer and worship experience. Have you recently examined the spontaneity of your own private and corporate worship? Do you notice on occasion that it is dry, impersonal, routine, meaningless? If so, question whether this sterility comes from your hesitation to bring your emotional self into the worship. Perhaps you relate to God only with logic and reason. Why? Maybe you have a long-standing anger toward God which you have tried to ignore. Maybe you suppressed the anger because you thought it was inappropriate. Now your worship is sterile because you don't dare allow any emotion to get expressed for fear that anger will come gushing out and catch you unprepared. It would free your spiritual self if you could trust God enough to be straightforward with that anger.

If your relationship with God is personal, then the same principles for gaining intimacy must be true. If you think of God as Person, and consider yourself made in God's image, then what choice have you but to relate to God in person-to-person terms? When anger occurs between you and God, you may be tempted to deny and suppress the anger, thinking that you are hiding it from God. Or you can choose to be aware of it, name it, and express it. If you try to hide your anger toward God, you can find yourself feeling distant and out of touch. Even more destructive would be expressing your anger toward God indirectly through the disguise of silence and withdrawal.

FitzSimons Allison has pointed out that one way in which sophisticated human beings get angry with God is with their silence. The old Hebrews felt free to shake their fists at God. Modern men and women, however, may feel this to be undignified, so they just ignore God. They scratch God off the list of people with whom they will relate. Allison, in his book *Guilt, Anger, and God,* notes that to be an atheist is one way of expressing anger toward God. An atheist acts as if God didn't exist.

To act as if another does not exist is a more hostile act than to slap his face. In the latter action one at least acknowledges his presence. The silent treatment is an extremely powerful weapon of aggression. With God, we are seemingly unable to hurt him in any other way. The only weapon we can use on him, as a vehicle for our anger at all the suffering he allows, is our silence. (P. 82)

If you believe in a God who cares for you and wants to relate to you, how could you defend hiding your anger? And what about trust? Don't you believe that God is trustworthy and that you are loved with steadfast love? Why would you hide your anger if you believe these things? The constructive option is to be open and honest with God about your anger. You can choose to share your anger with God, knowing that it will deepen your relationship.

Chapter 7
How Christians
Can Handle Anger

If Christian teaching leads people to handle (or mishandle) anger in such a manner that it becomes demonic, then it is obviously time for reevaluation not only of our teaching but of our practice. We must develop new ways of handling anger which enable Christians to be more loving and productive with the human experience of anger.

As Christians we are called to the "ministry of reconciliation" (II Cor. 5:18). As "ambassadors for Christ" (v. 20) we are to live and act in a way which proclaims the good news that Jesus the Christ "is our peace, who has made us both one, and has broken down the dividing wall of hostility" (Eph. 2:14). Paul reminds us that the reconciliation we have experienced in the Christ event is to be our "message of reconciliation" (II Cor. 5:19). We are to experience in ourselves and represent to others the unifying power of God's love.

We are quite aware of the antagonism, alienation, and animosity that characterize many human relationships. We also know that one of the major dynamics causing this disruption is the hostility that grows out of unresolved anger. If estrangement is to be transformed into reconciliation, it is imperative that we not only seek an understanding of the sources of anger and conflict (as we have done in preceding chapters) but also that we commit ourselves to a different way of handling anger. This new ethical approach must take seriously what we have learned from psychology and sociology as well as from the Bible and theology.

We can no longer accept the pious, unrealistic expectation that we Christians should not experience or express anger. We must accept that anger is a universal human experience, an emotional component of anxiety in the face of threats to our physical, social, psychological, and spiritual selfhood. To pretend that anger is not part of our human experience is foolish. From a faith standpoint, such pretending is a denial of our finitude and a distortion of God's creation. Understanding anger from a biblical perspective, particularly the life and work of Jesus, makes a new ethical stance imperative.

This chapter will describe a personal ethic which you, as an individual Christian, may use to help you confront anger more creatively and responsively. We will talk first about the necessity of raising our consciousness of anger when it occurs in us. Secondly, we will stress the importance of capturing and "naming" angry events for further evaluation. Thirdly, we will discuss interpreting and evaluating anger. Lastly, we will describe the process of taking responsibility for managing anger in ways that are consistent with Christian principles.

Expand Awareness

The first stage in handling your anger more creatively is *to increase your awareness* of angry feelings. You may want to read this first sentence again. It contradicts much that you have heard and read about how Christians should respond to anger.

We described earlier the numerous messages received from sermons, devotional literature, and family rules which indicate that being angry is not the loving thing to do. Therefore, we learned how to deny and suppress anger. Most of us have been taught *not* to pay attention to anger but instead to pretend it isn't occurring.

To consider expanding your awareness of anger (rather than

smiling and pretending it isn't there) may sound rather strange to you. It may seem heretical and unbiblical, but I hope our earlier discussions of Scripture and Christian doctrine will have convinced you otherwise.

Please read carefully. I have *not* said, "Christians should get more angry." I am not trying to create anger where none exists, but am trying to help us recognize what is already present. We have already demonstrated that all humans get angry, whether they admit they do or not. So the first step in handling anger more creatively is to recognize and accept the anger you do feel.

However strange it may sound, the best way *to decrease* your anger is *to increase* your awareness of the anger you do experience. Only by becoming more aware of your anger can you take the steps that will decrease the amount of anger you experience. So I am not advocating being more angry, but am trying to raise your consciousness about the importance of recognizing and labeling anger that occurs in day-to-day living. Why is this so necessary? Because, as we have discussed earlier, anger that goes unrecognized becomes destructive. You lose control over anger that you ignore. It moves into the inner recesses of your mind and creates problems.

What is ideal? Some say it would be ideal never to feel any anger. As we have seen, however, that is impossible. The ideal from my perspective is to develop self-awareness to the point where angry emotions would not escape your attention. From this ethical perspective, you work to develop your sensitivity to anger. Why? Heightening your awareness of anger allows you to finish the process. You cannot understand and evaluate anger, nor take ethical responsibility for resolving it creatively, if you are unaware of it! Anger that you ignore cannot be responsibly resolved.

Learning to recognize anger means changing long-standing patterns of reaction, which is not an easy task. If you are committed to a more creative Christian approach to anger, however, you can do it. Luckily, anger leaves a multitude of clues about its presence. Anger cannot come and go without leaving its mark. Let's discuss some of these clues and describe the telltale signs that give evidence of anger's presence in you.

PHYSICAL CLUES

Pay attention to what anger does to your body. Your body will be faithful to sound an alarm when you are threatened → anxious → angry. When anger is swallowed, it protests such unnatural treatment and goes down "kicking and screaming." Learn to read the physical symptoms that give testimony to the presence of angry emotion.

Probably the most common evidence is found in muscular action—such as grinding teeth, clenching fists, tightness in the back of the neck, and stomach cramps. The cardiovascular system may be affected, leading to headaches or pain around the heart. Indigestion, gas, heartburn, diarrhea, or constipation indicate that the gastrointestinal tract may have been victimized. How can you determine which physical symptoms you have when angry? The next time that you *know* you are angry, pay attention to your body. How does it function? Where does it hurt or cramp? Then the next time these symptoms appear (even though you are not consciously angry) you can cross-examine yourself about the presence of anger.

Playing detective in this manner is one way of familiarizing yourself with physical clues. For example, suppose you have indigestion? Maybe you drank too much coffee or ate too fast, *but* you could be irritated. When you have a headache, ask yourself what is going on. You might find that you stayed up too late, or stayed in the sun too long, *but* you might find that you were upset and did not realize the fact. Stiff neck? Diarrhea? Grinding your teeth? Do some investigative work on yourself. What has happened in the last few hours or days? Did you ignore something that threatened you and made you angry?

EMOTIONAL CLUES

Unidentified anger may express itself in your moods. Suppose you get up grouchy one morning. You may excuse this mood with some comment about "getting out of the wrong side of the bed" and try to forget it. But if you realize that the grumpiness may be a leftover from your emotional state yesterday, you can ask the question, "What was I feeling yesterday?" Suddenly you remember a disappointment you felt when a certain decision was made. You had not allowed yourself to be aware of the frustration and anger resulting from yesterday's disappointment (a *bitter* disappointment we call it). So the anger went unexpressed, and you pushed it inside. It could affect you all day. But if you recognize the clue, you can begin to understand the anger, work through it, and enjoy the rest of the day.

The "blues" are another mood clue. When you are "down in the dumps" it often means you have been angered. In this instance you are aiming the anger at yourself. If you can say to yourself, "If I'm depressed, I might be angry," and then explore what has been happening in the past several hours, days, or weeks, you might identify the angry feelings.

You are acquainted with other words that describe "bad moods": cranky, sullen, disagreeable, cross, touchy, ornery. A spouse or a child might ask why you are frowning, sulking, moping, huffy, or cantankerous. The chances are that any of these moods finds at its root some anger which you need to flush out and face forthrightly.

The words above describe moods. Other words serve as clues by describing negative emotion. If you label yourself as annoyed, hurt, jealous, frustrated, disappointed, aggravated, or irritated, then you can be sure that anger is happening. These words are synonyms for anger, but they call attention to the nature of the threat. "Jealous," for example, says you are threatened because somebody has something you want. "Frustrated" communicates that you are threatened because something is blocking your path or is in the way of your goals.

BEHAVIORAL CLUES

People who are insensitive to their negative feelings often develop behavioral patterns that signal their avoidance. These behaviors help keep negative feelings out of the mind. We are describing some actions that you may use in an attempt to escape from, or defend against, a threatening situation. Laughter is a common example.

> Barry is a thirty-one-year-old minister who laughs when he feels threatened. People call it a "nervous laugh." It is high-pitched and takes place in the throat, not in the chest or belly as when someone is really tickled. It takes place when things are tense, rather than in humorous situations. The laugh gives him a minute to figure out what response he is going to make to the threat.

I have known other people who have identified behavioral patterns such as getting something to eat, reaching for a cigarette, losing themselves in a book, or escaping into a television program. Acquaint yourself with behaviors you may use to sidestep and control your anger. When that behavior occurs, you can raise the question, "Am I angry?"

Sarcasm is always a good clue. If you notice that your humor has a sharp edge, let a light flash in your mind that signals, "Hey, I must be angry."

NAMING AND PRESERVING

Awareness of anger may come at a particular moment when it is impossible to continue the ethical process we are describing. That is, no time is available to reflect on, evaluate, or resolve it. A frustration or an irritation may occur minutes before company comes, just as your daughter leaves for school, on the way to church, or when an important long-distance call comes through. Given our traditional habit of ignoring anger, the usual result of such interruptions and delays is that we forget the incident, ignore the emotional response, and move on with the day's schedule. By the end of the day, the situation that produced the anger is all but gone from our awareness. The anger, of course, may still be floating around inside, or pushed into the storehouse where it can become more destructive than if we had been able to deal with it in the first place.

Because of this tendency to "forget," or lose touch with anger that we have experienced, it becomes important to capture this anger for further reflection. Our ethical approach, then, must include not only increased awareness of anger but also the *disciplined preservation* of the experience. The purpose for preservation, of course, is to have the experience available for evaluation, the next step in handling anger.

Whether the anger can be dealt with at the moment or must be preserved for later, it is important that the awareness be secured. This can best be done by naming and expressing it. By "naming," I refer to the process of honestly labeling what you are feeling inside as anger. An appropriate word (hurt, mad, frustrated, jealous, disappointed) is assigned to the angry feeling. Forcing ourselves to use a concept, a name, for this emotion will remind us that anger is happening and that we are ethically accountable for it. To name something is to acknowledge its existence. If you name the anger (even out loud to yourself), you will be less likely to let it slip out of sight. To name something in yourself not only helps you to recognize its existence but forces you to claim it as your own. Naming your anger facilitates taking responsibility for it.

Many people find that naming their negative emotion needs to be followed by expressing it to someone. In marriage, for example, if one spouse can name and express the negative feeling that is occurring, then the partner can be invited to participate in the evaluation and resolution of the anger. Or, if time or energy does not allow for immediate follow-up, the couple can plan a time when they will intentionally work through the angry experience by following the rest of the process described below.

UNDERSTANDING ANGER

The next stage in dealing with anger is to interpret and evaluate. It is not appropriate to continue thinking and reacting as if your anger is the problem. Anger is a symptom. As we have seen, it is an alarm which signals you that you are being threatened. To try to get rid of the anger, by counting to ten or trying to think a happy thought, is to lose an opportunity to understand yourself at a deeper level. Remember the story of Cain? The Lord asked Cain, "Why are you angry?" (Gen. 4:6). It would have given Cain a chance to handle his anger creatively if he had understood what really caused it. But he didn't, and his unresolved anger led him into sin.

The commitment to handle anger creatively calls for facing it head on and raising questions that could lead to self-discovery. When you become aware of anger, you can begin the search (Chapters 2 and 6 can serve as a guide). What was the anger all about? With whom or at what are you angry? Why are you angry? What is the threat? What part of yourself feels attacked or in danger? Explaining and interpreting the anger correctly is necessary to the last stage of taking ethical responsibility for resolution.

Notice that the evaluation focuses on the one who is angry, not on the persons or events that supposedly caused the anger. It is easy to blame other people, or groups, or events for our anger. However, this misses the real source which is inside our own self. This is not to say that other people and events are not involved; obviously they are part of the event that threatened our selves. But to understand our anger, to gain a psychological and theological explanation of its roots, calls for *self* evaluation.

Accepting Responsibility

You probably believe, as do most Christians, that taking responsibility for yourself is a necessary aspect of Christian existence. It is hoped that you include taking responsibility for your emotions, such as anger. Taking responsibility for your anger, of course, includes all the steps already discussed above: (1) increasing your sensitivity and awareness of anger, (2) being willing to name and preserve the anger for further study, and (3) developing an understanding of anger which helps you interpret and evaluate the anger accurately. Now what do you do after you understand the anger? The last step is to take responsibility for finding *appropriate* ways to express and resolve the anger. Ways that are loving and that, if possible, lead to reconciliation.

EXPRESSING ANGER

You may be wondering by now how we can talk so calmly and rationally about handling anger. You could be asking, "Hey, all this awareness and evaluation is okay, but when do we express the anger?" Good question! Actually, you may find yourself expressing the feelings at any point in this process.

A sharp, cutting remark could have been the clue that you were angry in the first place. In that situation you may have expressed the anger before you were aware of its presence. You may be a person who finds it necessary to concentrate on expressing anger *appropriately,* because your anger is so obvious that you don't have to worry about being aware of it or expressing it.

Suppose, however, that you are a person who has denied or ignored anger. Perhaps you are reading this book because of a new conviction that suppressed anger is causing some of your personal problems. You want to learn how to express your anger at the time you become aware of what is happening. Naming the emotion for yourself is helpful, but you must move to the point where you can risk saying it to the friend, family member, or business associate whose behavior has threatened you. The goal, in any case, would be to give expression to your feeling of anger so that reconciliation could begin.

CONFRONTATION

Anger can often be expressed directly at the source of the threat. This might mean a confrontation between you and the person or group with whom you are angry. It is to communicate clearly, "I am angry because . . ." or "It made me angry when . . ."

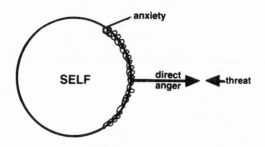

In Scripture we find models for seeking resolution through confrontation with the person whose behavior has threatened us. In Matthew 18, for example, Jesus gives these instructions:

> If your brother sins against you, go and tell him his fault, between you and him alone. If he listens to you, you have gained your brother. But if he does not listen, take one or two others along with you, that every word may be confirmed by the evidence of two or three witnesses. If he refuses to listen to them, tell it to the church; and if he refuses to listen even to the church, let him be to you as a Gentile and a tax collector. (Vs. 15–17)

To be sinned against is to be hurt, injured, discounted, ridiculed, and so forth. It is hard to imagine being sinned against without assuming that our personhood has been attacked in some manner. To be sinned against, therefore, is to be threatened → anxious → angry about what has taken place.

Please notice what Jesus did *not* say. He did *not* say, "If your brother sins against you, try to pretend you aren't angry. Be a nice person, just forget it and go on as if nothing had ever happened." Jesus knew what it was like to be sinned against. Judas, the Pharisees, and Herod treated him unjustly. Jesus knew what it was like to be angry and was obviously aware of the harm brought about by unresolved anger. So he instructs the disciples to take initiative in seeking reconciliation with their brothers and sisters. Feelings of hurt, frustration, and injustice must be openly expressed. If this is not successful, take several neighbors to help with the communication. If that fails, Jesus said, then involve the whole church in trying to settle the dispute and resolve the anger.

Jesus' interest in reconciliation is also obvious in the message that follows his famous words, "Every one who is angry with his brother shall be liable to judgment" (which we discussed in Chapter 3). Jesus said,

> So if you are offering your gift at the altar, and there remember that your brother has something against you, leave your gift there before the altar and go; first be reconciled to your brother, and then come and offer your gift. (Matt. 5:23–24)

Jesus realizes that when a person "harbors" or "nurses" anger, further conflict develops. He warns us to move toward reconciliation as soon as possible. He is referring to the Jewish belief that sacrifices at the Temple were not effective unless the persons offering such sacrifices were reconciled with their neighbors.

Why would Jesus say, "Your brother has something against you" instead of "You have something against your brother"? When you and I allow anger to fester inside, it is usually expressed (whether we want it to or not) in some disguised manner (see Chapter 4), such as the hurtful putdowns Jesus referred to in v. 22. So Jesus is probably thinking of the conflict and hostility we create in other people when we have handled our anger inappropriately. He reminds us to go to our neighbor and straighten things out. I think he is telling us to handle our anger in a more loving way. He wants us to be direct with it so reconciliation can take place. When anger is disguised and is expressing itself in destructive ways, reconciliation is very difficult.

SHARING ANGER

At times it is inappropriate, or even impossible, to express your anger directly to the person whose behavior is creating problems for you. For example, a person might not be fully accountable or knowledgeable about his or her impact on you.

> Lana and Howard came to me because they were "always picking at each other and hurting each other with nasty comments." They didn't understand why they were feeling alienated from each other. As we talked, I learned that they have a four-year-old handicapped child, named Eddie, who is able to live at home with them. Eddie was born with congenital birth defects that have impaired his physical coordination and his mental capacities. Eddie's needs are numerous. He does not always control his bowels and bladder. He gets very frustrated when his limited physical ability does not allow him to do what his friends can do. This frustration can generate temper tantrums. Since Eddie needs constant supervision, Lana and Howard must curtail their own work and leisure. To care for Eddie has many rewards because he is very lovable. However, his limitations do lead to behavioral patterns and confinement that are threatening to Lana and Howard's goals and ideals for Eddie and for themselves. Occasionally, of course, this produces anger.

What are Lana and Howard to do with their anger? To express it directly toward Eddie would not be appropriate (except for the amount of anger Eddie needs to hear to help him learn limits to his behavior). Eddie is not responsible for his birth, his handicap, or (at his age) his frustrations. But that doesn't keep Lana and Howard from feeling threatened and angry that they have a handicapped son whose presence limits their activity, demands much of their time, and threatens their ideal selves. To dump it on Eddie would be unethical. They felt badly about the anger, so both tried to keep it hidden. What happened, of course, is that each misplaced it on the other. In time, they learned to identify and then express their anger. Thankfully, their relationship was excellent and they were able to share a great deal with each other. But each also chose a trusted friend with whom to share the excess anger. Note the difference between sharing *with* and dumping *on*.

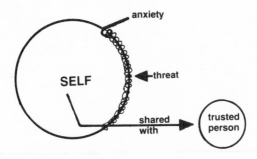

A second type of situation in which confrontation is difficult occurs when it seems too dangerous to express your anger toward the source of your anger. In fact, the danger may be part of the threat and generate some of the anger. This is often true in relationships where one person is dependent on another. When you are dependent on another person, it puts you in a risky position. What is the danger? If you express anger toward the person on whom you are dependent (such as an employer, a professor, a supervisor, your surgeon, your spouse, your parents, and so forth), you fear he or she might be offended and strike back by breaking the relationship. When you are dependent on that relationship, such a risk is difficult to take.

A third reason why you may not be able to express your anger toward the source of certain threats is that the person is not available. For example, you might be angry with a person who is dead:

> Bonnie was eighteen and very frustrated. She had been talking with me for three months about the anxiety she was experiencing as she became increasingly serious about her boyfriend. She had never been "in love" before, so had never entered into such an intimate relationship. The more involved they became, the more anxiety she experienced. She wanted to understand her anxiety and the occasional irrational outbursts of anger that she directed toward her boyfriend. Since I had known her family, it did not take us long to get to the root of her problem. Her father had been a problem drinker. He had abused Bonnie both sexually and emotionally during her early teens. She had been quite frightened of him during those years and kept her secret hatred of him tucked way down inside herself. In fact, she did not realize that her anger was so intense. Our conversations slowly uncovered the magnitude of her anger at the injustices she had suffered. Finally she was ready to confront him with her anger. She was very frustrated that this could not happen. He had frozen to death in a downtown alley the previous winter.

Bonnie had no choice but to share her anger with a trusted person. I was privileged to hear her lance the wound and spill the pent-up hostility. She also found it helpful to write a long letter to her deceased father which summarized what she had shared with me. Writing the letter gave her some sense of having confronted him personally. Soon her anxieties diminished, and the irrational anger toward her boyfriend subsided.

REDUCING ANGER

I have said throughout this book that all human beings experience anger and that those pretending not to are guilty of destructive hypocrisy. It is also true, however, that we can reduce the amount of anger we experience. I have also said that the Christian *should* feel threatened and get angry over some things. On the other hand, we are often threatened and angered by situations that don't have to threaten a maturing Christian.

REDUCING THREATS

One of the ways to take responsibility for your anger is to reduce the number of things that threaten you. When evaluating why you are angry, you will identify some threats that are unnecessary. When you ask, "Why am I threatened by that?" you will recognize that you are past the point in life where that particular person or event has to be threatening.

> Jane was constantly angry during visits home to see her family. "I go down there every time trying to be positive and not let them bother me, but each time I get upset and angry. I'm tired of it!" Jane was twenty-nine, the mother of two children, and married to a man who cared for her a great deal. She wondered how she could let her family upset her so much. (After we talked about the "threat model" described in Chapter 2, Jane evaluated her anger as follows.) "What gets to me are the constant put-downs. I've never done anything right, according to my mother!" Indeed, as Jane talked it was obvious that she never received any affirmation from her mother about how she looked, dressed, thought, or acted. Her father was withdrawn and, though never critical, offered no corrective to, nor protection from, the mother's criticism.

After some conversations, Jane realized she was giving her mother veto power over how she felt about herself. Her self-esteem was not very high (as one would imagine, since she grew up with such a critical parent). When she was a girl, it was natural for her to judge herself on the basis of her mother's observation, but she decided that at twenty-nine it was no longer necessary, and certainly not advisable, to give her mother such power. Slowly she began to believe the obvious acceptance and approval of her husband, friends, and church family. As she accepted these "votes," she reduced her mother's veto power. Finally she decided she didn't have to go home looking for that blessing which her mother and father never gave. When she did go home, she was not so vulnerable to her mother's criticism. Not surprisingly, when she did not need her mother's approval, she wasn't nearly as threatened by not receiving it. Not only was the anger toward her mother reduced but the part of that anger which spilled over onto her husband and the children was also reduced.

SEEKING A COUNSELOR

Whether or not you have been aware of your anger previously, you may be working hard to get at the root of your feelings. You may find, however, that no quick answers emerge. You may have examined your anger for many weeks and months without much success in understanding its causes. Perhaps you have gained some ground and are now able to identify why you are threatened in some situations. But in certain circumstances your anger makes no sense to you. When you ask, "Why did I get angry at that?" no answer is really satisfactory. Or perhaps you keep getting intensely angry over the same things. You know why you got angry, but you don't understand why the anger was so intense. What does this mean? It probably means that you are being affected by storehouse anger, which we described in Chapter 4. Storehouse anger may be related to specific traumatic events from the past, or it may be related to long-term relationships which, because of constant conflict, overdependency, or emotional abuse, continue to affect you today. In any case it is difficult to come to grips with anger from yesterday. This storehouse anger has probably been eating away at your insides for a long time. It has also been slowly poisoning your relationships.

What is the responsible action for you to take? I would suggest that from an ethical viewpoint your next step is to see a counselor. No, I don't think you are crazy. Few of the people I see are crazy, but they do want help in becoming what God wants them to become. They want to grow, develop, and mature, but aren't making the headway they want. I know you are concerned about the long-range impact your anger is having on your spouse, children, and friends. Because you love them, and because you take seriously Paul's admonition, "When you are angry, do not sin with it," I think you would like to find out what causes this anger. Only if you find out where it comes from will you be able to manage it creatively and keep from being unfair to your loved ones. Take time to ask people like your pastor, your physician, or your friends about the competent counselors in your locality. They may be pastoral counselors, psychologists, psychiatrists, social workers, or other mental health specialists. Make an appointment and tell them that you are struggling with handling your anger more creatively and want help in accomplishing that goal.

For Further Study

BOOKS FOR THE GENERAL READER

Allison, C. FitzSimons. *Guilt, Anger, and God.* Seabury Press, 1972.
Hauck, Paul A. *Overcoming Frustration and Anger.* Westminster Press, 1974.
Rohrer, Norman, and Sutherland, S. Philip. *Facing Anger.* Augsburg Publishing House, 1981.
Rubin, Theodore Isaac. *The Angry Book.* Macmillan, Collier Books, 1969.
Skoglund, Elizabeth R. *To Anger, With Love.* Harper & Row, 1977.
Southard, Samuel. *Anger in Love.* Westminster Press, 1973.
Walters, Richard P. *Anger: Yours and Mine and What to Do About It.* Zondervan Publishing House, 1981.

BOOKS FOR THE PROFESSIONAL READER

Ardrey, Robert. *The Territorial Imperative: A Personal Inquiry Into the Animal Origins of Property and Nations.* Atheneum Publishers, 1966.
Arendt, Hannah. *On Violence.* Harcourt Brace Jovanovich, 1969.
Bach, George R., and Goldberg, Herb. *Creative Aggression.* Doubleday & Co., 1974.
Bach, George R., and Wyden, Peter. *The Intimate Enemy.* William Morrow & Co., 1969.
Berkowitz, Leonard, ed. *Roots of Aggression: A Re-examination of the Frustration-Aggression Hypothesis.* Atherton Press, 1969.
Bowlby, John. *Separation: Anxiety and Anger,* Vol. II of *Attachment and Loss.* Basic Books, 1973. Ch. 17.
Buss, A. H. *The Psychology of Aggression.* John Wiley & Sons, 1961.

Fromm, Erich. *The Anatomy of Human Destructiveness,* New ed. Holt, Rinehart & Winston, 1973.

Lorenz, Konrad. *On Aggression.* Harcourt, Brace and World, 1966.

Madow, Leo. *Anger.* Charles Scribner's Sons, 1972.

May, Rollo. *Power and Innocence: A Search for the Source of Violence.* W. W. Norton & Co., 1972.

Megargee, Edwin I., and Hokanson, Jack E., eds. *The Dynamics of Aggression.* Harper & Row, 1970.

Montagu, Ashley. *The Nature of Human Aggression.* Oxford University Press, 1976.

Rochlin, Gregory. *Man's Aggression: The Defense of the Self.* Gambit, 1973.

Saul, Leon J. *Psychodynamics of Hostility.* Jason Aronson, 1976.

Tillich, Paul. *Love, Power and Justice: Ontological Analyses and Ethical Applications.* Oxford University Press, 1960.

Toch, Hans H. *Violent Men: An Inquiry into the Psychology of Violence.* Aldine Publishing Co., 1969.